SECOND CHANCES

Florida Pardons, Restoration of Civil Rights,
Gun Rights and More

What Others Say...

"The clemency process is one of the most emotional, significant to society and those who are directly affected, and misunderstood undertakings of Florida state government. Mr. Reggie Garcia has spent much of his legal career advising clients and state policymakers on clemency and closely observing its evolution over recent decades. For anyone who wants to understand how the king – now governor and cabinet – dispenses discretionary justice in Florida, this is the book to read."

— The Honorable Bob Graham, U.S. Senator 1987-2005; Governor of Florida 1979-1987 (January 15, 2015)

****

Reggie Garcia is "... an expert in clemency and parole cases."

— Sean Rossman, *Tallahassee Democrat* (July 21, 2014)

****

"I get many calls from people who made mistakes in their youth and as law-abiding adults want to regain firearms rights. Mr. Garcia's book gives the reader a good starting point with basic information to learn about clemency."

— Marion Hammer, Executive Director, Unified Sportsmen of Florida and past president of the National Rifle Association 1995-1998 (July 23, 2015)

****

"A man who *truly* seeks justice."

— Brian Tannebaum, Miami lawyer; author of *The Practice;* and past president of the Florida Association of Criminal Defense Lawyers (November 18, 2014)

****

"There is not a more qualified clemency/parole attorney in the State. And yet you took your time to educate me and introduce me to key players. Both [the inmate] and I are so grateful."

— Patti Velasquez, Delray Beach lawyer and mediator (December 1, 2014)

****

"It's the job of Reggie Garcia (JD '85) to win for his clients the rights and freedoms that no judge or jury can grant."

— Richard Goldstein, Editor/*UF Law*, in "Official Mercy," *UF Law* magazine (Fall 2011)

****

"We are so deeply touched by the pure passion, tireless dedication and absolute commitment that Reggie Garcia reflects every day to reverse a decades-old injustice."

— Ron Sachs, CEO/Sachs Media Group (August 24, 2014)

****

"If you want a passionate, capable, knowledgeable attorney on your case, you will find it in Reggie Garcia. He is qualified bar none to take your case before the Florida parole or clemency boards."

— Pat Bliss, retired paralegal (September 16, 2014)

Also by Reggie Garcia...

How to Leave Prison Early:
Florida Clemency, Parole and Work Release
(Laurenzana Press, January 30, 2015)

More Praise for How to Leave Prison Early

How to Leave Prison Early Update of Chapter 2,
and Appendix A: Clemency – Commutation of Sentence

SECOND CHANCES

Florida Pardons,
Restoration of
Civil Rights,
Gun Rights
and More

REGGIE GARCIA
Clemency Lawyer

Laurenzana Press

ISBN: 978-1-937918-85-9

Published by Laurenzana Press
PO Box 1220
Melrose, FL 32666 USA
www.LaurenzanaPress.com

Printed in the United States of America

Disclaimer

Nothing contained herein is to be considered as the rendering of legal advice, or the creation of an attorney-client relationship. Readers are responsible for obtaining such advice from their own legal counsel.

This book is intended for educational and informational purposes only. Any testimonials or past results included in this book are based on the specific circumstances of individual cases, and are not intended as a guarantee of future results.

Mary Jo Stresky, editor
Joni McPherson, book cover designer
Jean Boles, book interior designer

DEDICATION

Thank you to Florida's governors and members of the Florida Cabinet, who also serve as the Board of Executive Clemency, for granting executive clemency to certain convicted felons who *earned* mercy and a second chance.

Privileged to know ten Florida governors, and consider several as friends. I have presented clemency cases to four of them.*

Governor Claude Kirk, Jr.
(Republican, January 3, 1967–January 5, 1971)

Governor Reubin Askew
(Democrat, January 5, 1971–January 2, 1979)

Governor Bob Graham
(Democrat, January 2, 1979–January 3, 1987)

Governor Wayne Mixson
(Democrat, January 3, 1987–January 6, 1987)

Governor Bob Martinez
(Republican, January 6, 1987–January 8, 1991)

*Governor Lawton Chiles
(Democrat, January 8, 1991–December 12, 1998)

Governor Buddy MacKay
(Democrat, December 12, 1998–January 5, 1999)

*Governor Jeb Bush
(Republican, January 5, 1999–January 2, 2007)

*Governor Charlie Crist
(Republican, January 2, 2007–January 4, 2011)

*Governor Rick Scott
(Republican, January 4, 2011–present)

CONTENTS

INTRODUCTION

"All the great things are simple, and many can be expressed in a single word: freedom, justice, honor, duty, mercy, hope."

~ Sir Winston S. Churchill, Prime Minister of the United Kingdom (1940-1945; 1951-1955), is widely regarded as one of the greatest wartime leaders of the 20th century. Churchill also was an officer in the British Army, a historian, a writer, and an artist. He won the Nobel Prize in Literature, and was the first person to be made an honorary citizen of the United States.

My first book, *How to Leave Prison Early: Florida Clemency, Parole and Work Release,* was targeted to Florida prison inmates, their families, supporters and lawyers. It included the actual "how-to" steps for one type of executive clemency called a "commutation of sentence," and also for parole, work release and conditional medical release.

This purpose of this second book, *Second Chances: Florida Pardons, Restoration of Civil Rights, Gun Rights and More,* is to inspire and empower the reader by explaining the types of executive clemency available for convicted felons -- including full and conditional pardons, restoration of civil rights (RCR), firearm authority and more -- which can be granted by the four-member Florida Board of Executive Clemency comprised of the governor and members of the Florida Cabinet.

The target audiences are *all convicted felons who were adjudicated guilty in a state or federal Florida court*, regardless of whether they served time in prison or a county jail, or completed only probation or house arrest.

I included the powerful quote by Sir Winston S. Churchill because his six words -- *freedom, justice, honor, duty, mercy, hope* -- capture a great deal of what Americans strive for. As you will read throughout *Second Chances*, Executive Clemency is a grant of "mercy" and an increased opportunity for justice and hope.

Most people convicted of a first-time felony like drug possession or a property crime usually don't go to state prison or county jail. They typically...

- serve probation,

- pay fines, costs and restitution, and

- provide community service.

Convicted felons sentenced to one year or less serve their time in one of Florida's 67 county jails, and may or may not have probation once their jail sentence is completed. (County jails are operated by elected sheriffs who are independent constitutional officers, and often the most powerful elected officials in their counties.)

Convicted felons who serve longer sentences in one of Florida's 56 major state prisons usually get out after serving 85% of their sentence.

Eighty percent of the 101,000 Florida inmates in state prisons will eventually get out. In fact, one-third of state inmates will leave prison within the next 12 months. Inmates convicted of the most serious crimes may obtain probation after state prison, whereas most released inmates will not.

Just think about these facts for a minute: Regardless of their sentences, all convicted felons have lost valuable rights to:

- vote

- serve on a jury (for criminal or civil cases)

- run for elected office

- use, own, or possess a firearm.

Plus, it will be difficult, if not impossible, to get certain government, military, law enforcement, education, health care, and some sensitive private sector jobs. Most convicted felons also will have a difficult time getting certain state or federal occupational or professional licenses, and the jobs requiring these licenses.

What You'll Find In *Second Chances*

This book includes descriptions of the various types of clemency, case studies of successful clemency approvals, several bonus chapters, and a list of definitions to understand the sometimes complex paths to help a convicted felon become a productive citizen.

There's also a Call to Action chapter that tells you the information needed to get started.

And a bonus update to Chapter 2 and Appendix A of *How to Leave Prison Early,* with recent information on approvals of state and federal prison sentence commutations.

NOTE*:* Many thanks to the people who bought my first book, and to the readers who rated and "reviewed" it on Amazon, as it has garnered 26 "Five Gold-Star" customer reviews and a frequent Top 100 best seller ranking in the Criminal Law Procedure category. *How to Leave Prison Early* and/or its topics have been covered by more than 41 forms of media, including TV, radio, newspaper, magazine and digital.

Why I'm Qualified To Write This Book
I have:

- More than 20 years of experience presenting clemency cases to four Florida governors and numerous cabinet members of both political parties.
- Visited inmates and staff at 30 state prisons.
- Served as an expert witness for the Florida Bar in a clemency-related disciplinary proceeding in 2015.

- Been approved by the Office of Executive Clemency to handle death penalty clemency cases based on a 2014 law.

- Testified before Governor Rick Scott and the Florida Cabinet when the new clemency rules were approved in 2011.

- Met with the commissioners of the Florida Commission on Offender Review (FCOR) and their professional staffs on clemency and parole cases.

- Published legal articles in magazines and opinion editorials (op-eds) in newspapers related to clemency and parole.

- Given speeches to state associations, professional legal groups and community groups.

- Worked with lawyers and other clemency aides and parole investigators who do the nuts-and-bolts research, and make recommendations on whether to grant clemency.

- Appeared on national network and cable television, statewide programs, and local broadcast affiliate television stations.

- Been a legal commentator on the radio and published in magazines and newspapers and on websites.

- Worked with the Florida Department of Corrections' (FDOC) staff to obtain documents for clemency, parole and administrative prison matters.

- Presented to correctional officers and inmates in 2004 at the third largest federal women's prison in the country.

CHAPTER ONE

EXECUTIVE CLEMENCY EXPERIENCE

Since 1994, as a lawyer and state government lobbyist, I have assisted state prisoners, convicted felons, or other arrested clients with the following legal issues:

- Represented a former Miami police officer to obtain Restoration of Civil Rights (RCRs) for a federal drug conviction.

- Represented a small business owner from Alabama to obtain a full pardon for two 1988 drug convictions.

- After six years of working on a murder case, I argued it before the governor and Florida Cabinet.

- Assisted an inmate serving a life sentence for murder to obtain a clemency Request for Review.

- Assisted a Michigan contractor in obtaining a pardon for misdemeanor.

- Advocated for a Tampa Bay certified public accountant to obtain an expedited full pardon.

- Assisted an international business owner and registered sex offender to obtain a waiver and full pardon, negating his duty to register.

- Advocated for an inmate serving life in prison by presenting for him at a waiver hearing.

- Advocated for a Tampa Bay general contractor to obtain a Restoration of Civil Rights (RCR) without a hearing.

- Assisted a central Florida international business owner in obtaining a full pardon, including restoration of his firearm authority.

- Assisted a prison inmate convicted of DUI manslaughter in obtaining eligibility approval to seek a waiver and clemency.

- Assisted a prison inmate convicted of first degree murder and serving a life sentence to prepare for a national media network television interview.

- Advocated for an Illinois insurance agent to obtain specific authority to own, possess and use firearms.

- Assisted a major South Florida business owner to obtain an automatic RCR.

- Advocated for a Tampa Bay lawyer to obtain an automatic RCR, enabling him to seek re-licensure before the Florida Bar and the Supreme Court of Florida.

- Assisted an inmate to have his 14-year prison sentence for DUI manslaughter commuted to 8 years of time served—one of only 22 commutations approved by Governor Bush.

- Assisted a Polk County businessman to obtain a RCR.

- Assisted a Clearwater resident to obtain a full pardon.

- Assisted a Broward County public adjuster to obtain a RCR.

- Assisted a Brandon business owner to obtain (on the consent agenda) a full pardon.

- Assisted a Riverview electrician to obtain a RCR.

- Assisted an inmate to obtain approval for a waiver to seek a commutation of sentence.

- Assisted a Fort Myers general contractor and restaurant owner to obtain a RCR.

- Assisted a St. Pete general contractor to obtain a RCR.

- Assisted an Ohio business owner of a nursing home and pharmacy convicted of federal health care fraud to obtain a RCR without a hearing.

- Assisted a Tallahassee lawyer to obtain a RCR.

- Assisted a Miami lawyer to obtain a RCR.

- Assisted a Tampa business owner to obtain a RCR.

- Assisted an Illinois professional to obtain a pardon without firearm authority.

CHAPTER TWO

PERFORM A BACKGROUND INVESTIGATION ON YOURSELF (FACT QUESTIONS)

This book is called **Second Chances** for a particular reason: Because an inmate has to **earn** a second chance, and there's rarely a third chance.

This chapter discusses the 11 categories of information all convicted felons should know about themselves and support with written documentation.

Why?

- Because the Florida Commission on Offender Review (FCOR) staff that investigates all clemency applications will need most of it to prepare a "confidential case analysis," which will become the basis of a staff report that can impact the approval or denial of a clemency application.

- Because the three FCOR commissioners will need this information to make "advisory recommendations" to the Board of Executive Clemency.

- And because the applicant will want to provide it to demonstrate rehabilitation and establish credibility.

Misrepresenting any of this information, especially any criminal history, will almost always result in an application being denied. Therefore, I highly recommend disclosing *everything*, taking responsibility and showing accountability for one's actions, and expressing remorse.

The good news is the clemency application and documents submitted are confidential per **Clemency Rule 16**, which states:

Confidentiality of Records and Documents Due to the nature of the information presented to the Clemency Board, all records and documents generated and gathered in the clemency process as set forth in the Rules of Executive Clemency are confidential and shall not be made available for inspection to any person except members of the Clemency Board and their staff. Only the Governor, and no other member of the Clemency Board, nor any other state entity that may be in the possession of Clemency Board materials, has the discretion to allow such records and documents to be inspected or copied. Access to such materials, as approved by the Governor, does not constitute a waiver of confidentiality.

Yes, I suggest you *obtain, document and summarize* the following information. While it doesn't all need to be provided with the initial application, it should be provided during the investigation phase.

Clemency: Client Fact and Research Questions

I call this self-investigation the "No Surprise Rule" so that you, your lawyer (if you have one) and your family supporters are prepared for any questions. This information will greatly help you remember the details while presenting your case.

It will also help the FCOR staff prepare an investigation report, and the FCOR to make an advisory recommendation. In addition, it will help the governor and other board members judge your credibility and decide if you deserve mercy.

A. All Felony and Misdemeanor Convictions and Arrests (State and Federal)?

1. Crime
2. When
3. Where
4. Victims
5. Injuries

6. Deaths
7. Property Damage
8. Threats or Injuries to Law Enforcement Officials
9. Prior Expunction or Sealing
10. Registered Sex Offender or Predator
11. Restraining Orders or Injunctions

B. Prison, Jail, or Probation Served?

1. Sentence
2. When Completed
3. Department of Corrections Inmate Number
4. County Jail Inmate Number
5. Regular or Early Termination of Probation

C. All Jobs and Education?

1. Jobs
2. How Long
3. Salary
4. Commendations
5. Promotions
6. Degrees Completed (high school, college and/or graduate school)
7. Vocational or Other Certificates
8. Drug Tests

D. Finances, Regulatory or Disciplinary Matters?

1. Unsatisfied Judgments
2. Civil Lawsuits
3. Bankruptcy (personal or business)
4. Child Support
5. Regulatory Investigations, Fines, Cease and Desist Orders, Administrative or Civil Complaints
6. Local, State, or IRS Tax Investigations, Liens, Garnishments, Claims or Enforcement Actions
7. Any licenses Held, Achieved or Attained
8. Any License Denial, Suspension, or Revocation

9. Occupational City and County Licenses
10. Florida and Out-of-State Corporations, Partnerships, LLCs or other Business Entity
11. Credit Bureau Report
12. Collections Matters or Repossessions

E. Traffic Record?

1. DUI(s)
2. When
3. Where
4. Injuries
5. Deaths
6. Blood or Breath Alcohol Level (BAL)
7. Reckless or Careless Driving
8. Speeding Ticket(s) and Moving Violations
9. Accident or Civil Lawsuit
10. License Suspensions/Revocations

F. Family and Health Issues?

1. Married
2. How Long
3. To Who
4. Children
5. Divorce(s)
6. Child Support
7. Domestic Violence/Restraining Orders or Arrests
8. Mental Health
9. Baker Act
10. Alcohol and/or Substance Addictions

G. Church, Community, Volunteer Service and Contributions?

1. What
2. Where
3. When
4. Three Examples
5. Youth Sports

H. Character Letters?

1. Employer
2. Church or Community Leaders
3. Family Friends
4. Teachers
5. Law Enforcement
6. Probation Officer
7. Retired Judges
8. Supportive Victims

I. Anticipated Positions By?

1. Victim
2. Victim's Family
3. Presiding Judge
4. State Attorney
5. Probation Officer
6. Arresting Law Enforcement Agency

J. Media?

1. List all social media accounts (i.e., Facebook, LinkedIn, Twitter, Instagram, etc.).
2. Ever been mentioned in a newspaper, radio or TV story?

K. Other Important Information?

1. Anything law enforcement may already know
2. Public records from the clerk's office(s) and other government agencies
3. Things that help
4. Things that may not help, but should be acknowledged and explained
5. Everything you can think of!

CHAPTER THREE

EXECUTIVE CLEMENCY – THE BASICS AND 25 PROACTIVE STEPS

Seeking Mercy and Justice for Convicted Felons

Florida Governor Rick Scott, and three statewide elected members of the Florida Cabinet acting as the Board of Executive Clemency (the Board), unanimously approved new clemency rules effective March 9, 2011[1]. The following major changes applied to all pending applications at the time and future applications for:

Restoration of Civil Rights

The person must file an application and be crime-free for at least five years to be eligible for approval "without a hearing." For the 35 most serious offenses, the applicant must be crime-free for seven years, and must be approved at a clemency hearing in Tallahassee.

Full Pardon and Firearm Authority

The ten-year waiting period for a full pardon, and the eight-year waiting period for firearm authority, are the same. However, these time periods can no longer be "waived" as these major changes replaced the April 2007 rules, and are "intended to emphasize public safety and ensure that applicants desire clemency and demonstrate they are unlikely to re-offend."[2]

---

[1] Unless otherwise noted, all rule citations are to the Florida Rules of Executive Clemency (Fla.R.Ex.C.), effective March 9, 2011.
[2] Governor Scott's Remarks Prepared for Delivery, March 9, 2011.

Who Can Benefit From Clemency?

A convicted felon may seek firearm authority for personal and family safety reasons, business protection or recreational hunting.

Florida and certain out-of-state residents who have a previous felony conviction -- and have completed their prison or jail sentence or probation -- often need information to seek clemency approval for Restoration of Civil Rights (RCR), a full pardon or firearm authority.

Clemency approval by the Board could be of valuable assistance to obtain certain jobs, business or professional opportunities, state licenses, bonds, government contracts and/or security clearances.

Forms of Executive Clemency

Executive Clemency is a power vested in the governor by the Florida Constitution of 1968.[3] Clemency is an act of mercy absolving the individual upon whom it's bestowed from any part of the punishment that the law imposes.[4]

Following are the eight types of clemency:
1. Full Pardon
2. Pardon without firearm
3. Pardon for misdemeanor
4. Commutation of sentence
5. Remission on fines and forfeiture
6. Specific authority to own, purchase or use firearms
7. Restoration of civil rights
8. Restoration of alien status

Hearings and Approval "Factors"

As previously stated, the Board is comprised of Governor Scott and the three statewide elected members of the Florida Cabinet (as of this writing, Attorney General Pam Bondi, Chief Financial

---

[3] Art. VI, § 8 (a), Fla. Const.
[4] Fla. R. Ex. C. 1 Statement of Policy.

Officer Jeff Atwater, and Commissioner of Agriculture Adam Putnum).

The Board meets four times a year in Tallahassee to hear public testimony and vote on clemency applications. And through its staff, periodically to consider "Requests for Review."

Approval by the governor and two members of the Board is required to obtain any form of clemency[5]. Approval by the governor and one member of the Board is required to obtain a Request for Review, a condition-precedent to a commutation of sentence.

The Board will consider these six factors when determining whether to grant an applicant clemency:[6]

1. The nature of the offense;
2. Whether the applicant has any history of mental instability, drug or alcohol abuse;
3. Whether the applicant has any subsequent arrests, including traffic offenses;
4. The applicant's employment history;
5. Whether the applicant is delinquent on any outstanding debts or child support payments; and
6. Letters submitted in support of, or opposition to, the grant of executive clemency.

Informally, additional common sense criteria are:

• Is the applicant remorseful?

• Has the applicant apologized to the victim?

• Has the applicant learned their lesson?

---

[5] Art. VI, § 8 (a), Fla. Const.
[6] Information and Instructions for Applying for Clemency per Form ADM 1501.

- Has the applicant ever reoffended?

- Is the applicant a public safety risk?

- Is the applicant currently a productive law-abiding citizen and taxpayer?

- If the application is approved, will that help the applicant get a better job, start or grow a business, get more education, hire more people, or help others be productive?

- Is there a strong spouse or other family member to help be an enforcer of the criteria?

Expediting a Case for "Exceptional Merit" Per Rule 17

Rule 17 provides that in cases of "exceptional merit," any member of the Board may place a case on an upcoming agenda for consideration. Historically this was infrequently done, so only time will tell if and when Board members exercise this prerogative.

Also unclear is if Rule 17 will be used to expedite only pending applications. Or whether otherwise time-ineligible persons can be considered.

No State Application or Court Document Fees

Currently there is no state fee or cost to seek clemency. Likewise, Florida law provides that the certified copies of court records required for all types of clemency shall be furnished by the clerk of court to the applicant *free of charge* and without delay.[7]

The free court records specifically include the criminal "information" or indictment (also called "charging documents"), judgment and sentence.

Applications and the clemency rules can be obtained by calling the Office of Executive Clemency at 850-488-2952 or from The Florida Commission on Offender Review website: https://www.fcor.state.fl.us/.

---

[7] § 940.04, Fla. Stat. (2015).

25 Proactive Steps That Can Make a Difference

Every case has different needs. But these 25 proactive "how-to" steps help increase chances of success for a clemency applicant:

Phase 1:

☐ 1. Review the felony conviction documents, including the police report, probable cause affidavit, charging instrument (direct filed information or grand jury indictment), judgment, and sentence, autopsy report, court transcripts, appellate record and legal briefs.

☐ 2. Review the Florida Department of Law Enforcement (FDLE) criminal history.

☐ 3. Review any public records related to the inmate from the Florida Department of Corrections (FDOC).

☐ 4. Review the complete driving record from Florida Department of Highway Safety and Motor Vehicles (FDHSMV).

☐ 5. Determine and confirm with the clemency staff the applicant's clemency eligibility.

☐ 6. Interview the applicant and family.

☐ 7. Interview the plea, trial and appellate lawyers.

☐ 8. Determine the legal and political viability of the case.

Phase 2:

☐ 9. Obtain from the applicable Clerk of Circuit Court certified copies of court records.

☐ 10. Prepare and hand deliver the clemency application and certified records.

☐ 11. Prepare an advocacy letter describing mitigating factors, rehabilitation since the conviction, and the six approval "factors."

☐ 12. Assist to obtain character and support letters.

☐ 13. Determine if the case has "exceptional merit."

☐ 14. Meet with the governor's clemency lawyers and other clemency aides to answer questions and advocate for approval.

Phase 3:

☐ 15. Prepare for the applicant's interview with the parole examiner.

☐ 16. Provide information to, and meet with, the three members of the Florida Commission on Offender Review to encourage a positive advisory recommendation.

☐ 17. Coordinate with the applicant's supporters.

☐ 18. Provide continuing legal counsel and advice.

☐ 19. Provide written clarification of any issues raised during the investigation.

☐ 20. Review the Confidential Case Analysis and advisory recommendation.

☐ 21. Contact the governor's legal counsel and other clemency aides prior to the clemency board meeting.

☐ 23. Select witnesses, and otherwise prepare for and attend the clemency hearing.

☐ 24. Coordinate any follow-up communications required during the process or after the clemency meeting, including obtaining the letter or executive order describing the decision.

☐ 25. Regardless of the decision, write to thank the governor, cabinet members and their clemency aides.

This list may feel overwhelming, so just approach it one step at a time. Please be patient, as seeking justice and mercy isn't a quick or easy process.

CHAPTER FOUR

FULL AND CONDITIONAL PARDONS

The most famous federal clemency pardon in history was when President Gerald Ford granted a "full, free and absolute pardon" to former President Richard Nixon who was facing potential Articles of Impeachment by the U.S. House of Representatives for obstruction of justice for his Watergate-related crimes.

The presidential pardon was granted on September 8, 1974, one month after Nixon resigned and **before** he was impeached by the House, tried by the U.S. Senate or charged with any federal crimes. The pardon was controversial, and contributed to President Ford's close loss in 1976 to former Georgia Governor, Jimmy Carter.

Arguably the most "infamous" federal presidential pardon in recent history was by President Bill Clinton when he pardoned Marc Rich, an international fugitive charged with 51 counts of tax fraud, and was listed as the number six international fugitive on the U.S. Department of Justice's most-wanted list.

Again, the pardon was controversial, and among 140 pardons President Clinton granted on his final day in office on January 20, 2001.

As of July 13, 2015, President Barack Obama has granted 64 Full Pardons in six-and-a-half years.

Article II, Section 2, of the United States Constitution, states in part...

> "the President ... shall have power to grant reprieves and pardons for offences against *the United States, except in cases of Impeachment."* (Clause 1)

The presidential power to grant reprieves (like prison commutations) and pardons is essentially absolute. Congress and the federal courts have no meaningful oversight or role. Nor can a future president rescind a prior president's decision.

Like the federal Constitution, the Florida Constitution gives the governor (with the consent of two members of the Florida Cabinet) executive power to grant clemency as an act of mercy. The granting of Executive Clemency in Florida, including a Full Pardon, doesn't involve the courts or the Florida Legislature.

In Florida, a Commutation of Sentence is the hardest type of clemency to obtain because it releases an inmate early from prison. The second hardest type of clemency is called a "Full Pardon" because it also restores firearm authority.

> **Per Rule 4.I.A.**: *A full pardon unconditionally releases a person from punishment and forgives guilt for any Florida convictions. It restores to an applicant all of the rights of citizenship possessed by the person before his or her conviction, including the right to own, possess, or use firearms.*

An applicant must wait ten (10) years from the conclusion of prison or probation, **whichever is last**, before seeking a Full Pardon. Probation can be instead of or after state prison.

In their first terms between 2011 and 2014, Governor Rick Scott and the three members of the Cabinet approved 88 Full Pardons and 3 conditional pardons without firearm authority.

I successfully argued and helped clients obtain Full Pardons during this period for two out-of-state business owners who committed felonies when they were younger.

Obtaining a Full Pardon has many benefits, including:

- Helping a felon get state or federal licenses
- Getting security clearances
- Procuring government contracts
- Providing for potentially better jobs
- Allowing for volunteer opportunities at schools or nonprofit organizations

A Full Pardon is the ultimate "**second chance**" where the state's top four elected officials recognize that someone has turned their life around and is now a productive citizen.

Although I didn't handle these cases, the following are two noteworthy Florida pardons that generated a great deal of media attention:

- Governor Reubin Askew was Florida's 37th governor, serving 1971-1979. In 1975, joined by three members of the Florida Cabinet he pardoned Freddie Lee Pitts and Wilbert Lee, two African-American death row inmates falsely convicted of the 1963 murders of two gas station attendants in Port St. Joe (Gulf County), Florida.

Governor Askew also commuted their prison sentences, and ordered them released after they had served 12 years. (In 1998, Gov. Lawton Chiles and the Florida Legislature awarded Mr. Pitts and Mr. Lee $500,000 each in a compensation "claims bill" for their wrongful incarceration.)

- Governor Charlie Crist was Florida's 41st governor, serving 2007-2011. In 2010, he and the Florida Cabinet unanimously pardoned singer Jim Morrison (of the famous band, The

Doors). Even though he was dead, the posthumous pardon was for Morrison's 1969 conviction for "indecent exposure and open profanity" during a Miami concert.

Conditional and Other Pardons

Rule 4 gives the governor "unfettered discretion" to deny clemency, and to grant it with the consent of two cabinet members.

A pardon also can be approved without firearm authority (Rule 4.I.B.); for a misdemeanor conviction (Rule 4.I.C); and even if adjudication was "withheld" -- meaning there was no formal finding of guilt, so the person is not a convicted felon and did not lose their civil rights (Rule 5-A).

Conditions can be attached to the grant of a pardon, including periodic substance or alcohol testing, and virtually anything else that tailors the approval to past crimes with certain restrictions on future activities.

Between 2011-2014, three pardons without firearm authority were approved, and seven pardons for misdemeanors were approved.

Clemency is Different Than "Expunction" or Sealing of Criminal History Information

A full pardon will not expunge or facilitate the expungement of a criminal record. Please contact the Florida Department of Law Enforcement at seal-expunge@fdle.state.fl.us. Or call 850/410-7870 to obtain an "Application for Certification of Eligibility" to seek expunction or sealing of a criminal history record. There's a $75 fee, and specific and limited eligibility criteria established by Florida law. [8]

---

[8] § 943.0585, Fla. Stat. for expunction (2015); § 943.059, Fla. Stat. for sealing (2015).

If the FDLE approves eligibility, an applicant must then file a petition in the circuit court where the criminal proceeding originally occurred to seek court approval.

Expunction is when a criminal history record is physically destroyed so no one would have access to it. **Sealing** is when a criminal history record becomes inaccessible to any person not having a legal right to access criminal history records, or the information contained or preserved in those records.

Police, military, local, state and federal government agencies continue to have a legal right to access sealed records, while most employers and the public generally do not.

Expunction or Sealing Eligibility will not occur if you:

- Have a conviction (was adjudicated guilty) for any criminal offense (including traffic, misdemeanor, or felony);

- Committed one of 22 serious crimes, even if you received a "withhold of adjudication;"

- Were adjudicated delinquent as a juvenile of certain charges;

- Violated probation or community control resulting in the initial withhold of adjudication being converted to an adjudication of guilt;

- Have an open case, unpaid restitution or court costs; or

- Have every previously had a record sealed or expunged in any jurisdiction, including another state.

In 1999, the Board of Executive Clemency specifically declared that the granting of a Full Pardon does not remove a condition of ineligibility for expunging or sealing a criminal history record, and directed FDLE accordingly.

A FULL PARDON CASE STUDY: Fighting and Underage Drinking = Two Quick Felony Convictions

In 1992, a young teenager punched a man in a St. Petersburg Subway restaurant to help his friend who was getting beat up by several young men. He was arrested and charged with *felony* aggravated assault.

Why?

This case shows the discretion and powers our police officers and prosecutors can exercise. The case was arguably self-defense because he intervened to help a friend in a public place. At worst, he should have been charged with *misdemeanor* battery, a less serious crime. He was put on probation and adjudication was withheld, which meant the judge made no formal finding of guilt and the young man was *not* a convicted felon.

However, while still on probation the young man was at a party and engaged in under-age drinking. Panicking when the police arrived, he ran. And while jumping over a fence, his feet inadvertently kicked the officer who was chasing him. He was charged with *misdemeanor* underage drinking and *felony* resisting arrest *with violence*.

Again, I think he was over-charged by the police and prosecutors. The new charges meant he also violated probation on the first charge (the fighting at the Subway restaurant), so he was adjudicated guilty on that felony charge and on the two new charges. He now had two felony convictions before he was 21 years old.

There are thousands of these types of stories in Florida, especially involving minors and young adults. He was at a critical juncture in his life. Without much parental or community support, he straightened up, made great grades in college and earned bachelor's and master's degrees in accounting.

So, why did he need a Full Pardon?

In his late 30s, married with two young children and with a great job, he was the chief financial officer of a real estate investment trust business. The company was raising funds in the New York capital markets, and had to disclose to investors my client's and other officers' backgrounds. The man also wanted to volunteer at his children's school and with sports activities.

We filed a clemency application and got two cabinet members to agree to expedite it under Rule 17, where in cases of "exceptional merit" the governor or any member of the Florida Cabinet can expedite a case. This is rarely done.

In December 2010, the man received a unanimous Full Pardon.

Now in his early 40s, he continues to be an outstanding accountant, financial professional, citizen, taxpayer, homeowner, husband, father and community volunteer and leader.

This was a good clemency result for all the right reasons. Many of the pardons I've helped obtain, or just witnessed during the quarterly hearings, involve similar success stories where people have cleaned up their act and earned a "**second chance**."

CHAPTER FIVE

SPECIFIC AUTHORITY TO OWN, POSSESS OR USE FIREARMS

Florida law, § 790.23, makes it a second degree felony punishable up to 15 years in state prison for a convicted felon to own, possess or control any firearm or ammunition. Subsection (2) of this law says this prohibition "shall not apply to a person convicted of a felony whose civil rights *and* firearm authority have been restored."

As described later in this chapter, my first clemency case in 1994 was a firearms case. Since then, and especially the last few years, I get many calls, letters and emails from convicted felons who want (or arguably need) firearms to:

- Protect their family, employees and property.

- Go hunting with friends, relatives, customers or clients.

- Inherit a parent's or grandparent's gun collection.

- Use for certain law enforcement, military or private security jobs.

Clemency Rule 4.1.F. states:

"The Specific Authority to Own, Possess, or Use Firearms restores to an applicant the *right to own, possess, or use firearms, which were lost as a result of a felony conviction.*

Clemency Rule 5. D. states:

"A person may not apply for the specific authority to own, possess, or use firearms unless he or she has completed all sentences imposed for the applicant's most recent felony conviction and all conditions of supervision imposed for the applicant's most recent felony conviction have expired or been completed, including but not limited to, parole, probation, community control, control release, and conditional release, *for a period of no less than eight (8) years*.

The applicant may not have outstanding detainers, or any pecuniary penalties or liabilities which total more than $1,000 and result from any criminal conviction or traffic infraction. In addition, the applicant may not have any outstanding victim restitution, including, but not limited to, restitution pursuant to a court order or civil judgment, or obligations pursuant to Chapter 960, Florida Statutes. Persons convicted in a federal, military, or out-of-state court are not eligible to apply."

Due to federal firearms laws, the Clemency Board will not consider requests for firearm authority from individuals convicted in federal or out-of-state courts. In order to comply with the federal laws, a Presidential Pardon or a Relief of Disability from the Bureau of Alcohol, Tobacco and Firearms must be issued in cases involving federal court convictions. A pardon or restoration of civil rights with no restrictions on firearms must be issued by the state where the conviction occurred.

In their first terms between 2011-2014, the governor and clemency board approved 88 Full Pardons, which **includes** firearm authority. In addition, 78 other clemency applications were approved for only firearm authority (not as part of a Full Pardon).

A Gun Rights Case Study: My First Clemency Case

It seems like yesterday when Tampa lawyer Marcelino J. "Bubba" Huerta called in 1994, and asked me to help a Tampa small business owner obtain firearm authority. All convicted felons lose this right. The client had some minor felony drug and other convictions, but had also been a crime victim.

The Florida Parole Commission's (now called the Florida Commission on Offender Review) advisory recommendation was negative.

There was damaging, inaccurate and incomplete information in the court records, so we had to investigate and clarify all the facts and legal issues. (This case and many subsequent ones are why I developed the investigative and fact questions described in Chapter 2.)

The client owned a small retail business in a high crime area of north Tampa, and handled a significant amount of cash daily. His residence was above the business, so the firearm was to protect his employees, customers and family members.

After conducting our investigation we met with all of the clemency aides to the governor and six cabinet members. (In 2003, after passage of a constitutional amendment, the Florida Cabinet was reduced to the current three members.) Governor Lawton Chiles and the Florida Cabinet approved the firearm authority application.

These cases started my interest in, and focus on, helping convicted felons through the clemency process and later the parole process.

The U.S. Constitution and Federal Law

The Second Amendment

The Second Amendment to the U.S. Constitution guarantees the right of the people to "keep and bear arms." It was adopted on December 15, 1791, among the first ten amendments contained in the Bill of Rights. The Second Amendment guarantees:

> *A well-regulated militia, being necessary to the security of a free state, <u>the right of the people to keep and bear arms</u>, shall not be infringed.* (underline added for emphasis)

The Gun Control Act of 1968, as amended

Passage of the Gun Control Act was initially prompted by the assassination of President John F. Kennedy in 1963.[9]

The deaths of Reverend Martin Luther King, Jr. in April 1968, and U.S. Senator Robert F. Kennedy in June 1968, renewed efforts to pass the bill[10]. House Resolution 17735, known as the Gun Control Act, as amended, was signed into law by President Lyndon B. Johnson on October 22, 1968[11], banning mail order sales of rifles and shotguns and prohibiting most felons, drug users and people found mentally incompetent from buying guns[12] [13].

Key Sections of the 1968 Gun Control Act:

§922(g) makes it unlawful for any person ...

> (1) who has been convicted in any court of, a crime punishable by imprisonment for a term exceeding one year; or

> (9) who has been convicted in any court of a misdemeanor crime of domestic violence;

> . . . to possess any firearm or ammunition.

Others prohibited from firearm possession or ownership include: Fugitives, certain drug users, people adjudicated "mentally

---

[9] Jon Michaud, The Birth of the Modern Gun Debate, The New Yorker (July 6, 2014), http://www.newyorker.com/books/double-take/the-birth-of-the-modern-gun-debate

[10] Steven Rosenfeld, The NRA once supported gun control, Salon Media Group (July 7, 2014),
http://www.salon.com/2013/01/14/the_nra_once_supported_gun_control/

[11] 553-Remarks Upon Signing the Gun Control Act of 1968 (October 22, 1968), http://www.presidency.ucsb.edu/ws/?pid=

[12] Kevin Dolak, Gun Debate Spurred by Kennedy Assassination Rages on Today, ABC News (July 7, 2014), http://abcnews.go.com/US/gun-debate-spurred-kennedy-assassination-rages-today/story? id=20677433 Hyperlink in print

[13] U.S. gun control: A History of tragedy, legislative action, CBS News (July 7, 2014), http://www.cbsnews.com/news/us-gun-control-a-history-of-tragedy-legislative-action/

defective," certain aliens, former military members given a dishonorable discharge, anyone who has renounced their citizenship, convicted stalkers, and others deemed a danger to children.[14]

§921(a)(20) describes the remedies available for someone with a felony conviction.[15]

§921(a)(33)(B)(ii) describes the remedies available for someone with a conviction for misdemeanor crime of domestic violence.[16]

As you can see, firearm authority is a combination of state and federal law but rehabilitated, non-violent felons have an opportunity to earn mercy and a **second chance**.

---

[14] 18 U.S. Code § 922(g)(2)-(8).
[15] 18 U.S. Code § 921(a)(20).
[16] 18 U.S. Code § 921(a)(33)(b)(ii).

CHAPTER SIX

RESTORATION OF CIVIL RIGHTS: VOTE, SERVE ON A JURY OR SEEK ELECTED OFFICE

A disproportionate number of convicted felons are minorities. But many also are young adults, working poor, from rural areas and small towns, and from every city in Florida.

Increasingly, convicted felons are *our* family members, neighbors, school friends, business owners, skilled workers, and former or current professionals of every race, gender, ethnicity, religion and socio-economic group.

Felons made bad decisions, committed crimes, got arrested, and were convicted at least once and often multiple times. Based on the calls and emails I receive, many of the people who got convicted made bad choices and decisions, usually at a young age.

Most couldn't afford good legal counsel, or were too young or under-educated to understand the gravity of the legal proceedings, or how to make informed decisions. Many say they had no idea a "no contest" or guilty plea would create life-long obstacles, especially for employment.

With nearly 101,000 inmates in 56 state prisons in Florida, approximately one-third will return to society in the next 12 months. Another 142,000 felons are on "community supervision" more commonly known as "probation" (probation can be instead of or after prison or county jail).

With thousands more inmates leaving federal prison and Florida's 67 county jails every year, we as citizens and taxpayers should help these felons get jobs and transition back to being law-abiding and self-sustaining citizens. (Chapter 13 goes into more detail on the transition and re-entry processes.)

Many of the clemency applicants I've represented are business owners or professionals who had a prior felony conviction. Now they have a roadblock to obtaining local, state or federal licenses, security clearances, government contracts, better jobs and even volunteer opportunities with nonprofits or schools.

Clemency is the ultimate **second chance**, where the state's four top elected officials recognize that someone has turned their life around. RCR is usually the first step and the easiest type of clemency to obtain.

It's an incredible achievement in the third largest state in the country to say "the governor and Florida Cabinet granted me restoration of my civil rights or any type of clemency." You almost have to be there to believe it. People openly weep when they're successful, because in many cases they've devoted years of their life ... and their blood, sweat and tears ... to redeeming themselves.

Restoration of Civil Rights (RCR)

Convicted felons lose the rights to vote, serve on a jury and run for elected office. In order to get these rights restored, a person must file an application for "restoration of civil rights" (RCR). They must have been 1) crime-free for at least *five years* to be eligible for approval "without a hearing"; 2) for the 35 most serious offenses, be crime-free for *seven years*; and 3) must be approved at a hearing. These waiting periods were approved by the governor and Florida Cabinet serving as the "Board of Executive Clemency."

Clemency approval by the Board could be of valuable assistance to obtain certain jobs, business or professional opportunities, state licenses, bonds, government contracts and/or security clearances.

Though convicted felons also lose the right to own, possess or use firearms, RCR does not restore that right. Restoration of firearm authority is a separate type of clemency.

In March 2011, Governor Rick Scott and the Clemency Board made major rule changes which **created two distinct categories of RCR eligibility:**

- Most significant, the rules now require the applicant to wait *five years* after conclusion of prison or probation to be eligible and the person must actually submit an application.

- In addition, felons convicted of 35 of the most serious crimes are *ineligible* for approval without a hearing. As before, the applicant must complete their sentence and conditions of supervision, pay restitution, have no outstanding detainers, and not have any new arrests or convictions during the *waiting period*.

RCR "Without a Hearing"

Rule 4.I.G. governs Restoration of Civil Rights, which "restores to an applicant all of the rights of citizenship – voting, serving on a jury, and seeking elected office – in Florida enjoyed before the felony conviction, <u>except</u> the specific authority to own, possess or use firearms." Rule 9.A. establishes who is eligible for restoration of civil rights without a hearing.

RCR "With a Hearing"

Meeting quarterly, the Board considers approximately 300 to 400 clemency cases per year.

Per Rule 10.A. there's a *new seven-year waiting period* for 35 of the most serious Florida crimes and any offense committed out-of-state or for a federal conviction (that would be an offense listed in Rule 9.A).

The 2011 rules will result in more hearings. But applicants will still have an open path to demonstrate rehabilitation and earn the opportunity for RCR.

The board will consider these six factors when determining whether to grant an applicant clemency:

1. The nature of the offense.
2. Whether the applicant has any history of mental instability, drug or alcohol abuse.
3. Whether the applicant has any subsequent arrests, including traffic offenses.
4. The applicant's employment history.
5. Whether the applicant is delinquent on any outstanding debts or child support payments.
6. Support or opposition letters.

As before, the applicant must complete his or her sentence and conditions of supervision, pay restitution, have no outstanding detainers, and not have any new arrests or convictions during the waiting period.

During their first terms between 2011-2014, Governor Scott and the Clemency Board approved 1,335 RCR "without a hearing" (based on an email dated 9/2/15 from Clemency Coordinator Julia McCall), and another 215 were approved at quarterly hearings.

Even if or when you do obtain a RCR, there are things that don't change. For example, when a loved one or friend dies, a convicted felon cannot serve as the "personal representative" (sometimes called an "executor") of the deceased's estate, even if their Last Will and Testament purports to appoint the felon. Per Florida law § 733.303(1)(a), RCR does not remove this disability.

However, the convicted felon's status (with or without RCR) does not preclude being an inheritance beneficiary or affect the right to challenge a will.

A RCR CASE STUDY: A Young Miami Police Officer Commits a Serious Crime

Miami, 1989. Cocaine and cash were everywhere. Though he wasn't one of the ringleaders, a 29-year-old police officer reluctantly agreed to stash 51 kilos of stolen cocaine in his home. Yes, the coke that was supposed to go to the police station's evidence room.

It was stupid, illegal and dangerous.

The officer became part of the infamous "Miami River Cops Jones Boatyard Rip-off" case that made news headlines, ruined careers, and changed lives.

After emigrating from Cuba, and proudly becoming a naturalized U.S. citizen, he served with distinction as a U.S. Marine and was honorably discharged. With a dream to serve and protect his new country and community, he started well but fell to a temptation for quick money. Within a few days he regretted his decision, donated the crime's profits to his church, and confessed to law enforcement that he had been a participant in the crime.

The young police officer was fired, and was arrested and convicted of a serious federal crime called Conspiracy to Possess with Intent to Distribute in Excess of One Kilogram of Cocaine. Sentenced to five-and-a-half years in federal prison, he completed probation afterwards in 1995.

Then what?

With a devoted wife and several children, a strong faith, and a great work ethic at a family-owned business, he got the **second chance** that most convicted felons never get.

He was never arrested again. In fact, during the last 20 years he has been a remarkable model citizen, married for 38 years and is a tremendous role model to his sons and grandsons, fellow church members and to others in the community. Now 58 years old, he employs 13 workers at two successful small, family-owned businesses.

In 2015, Governor Scott and the Florida Cabinet unanimously granted him his RCR.

What are the lessons here?

First, an important legal point: Because he had a federal conviction, the Florida governor can *only* grant RCR. If and when he wants a Full Pardon or firearm authority, he must apply to the U.S. Department of Justice and get the president's approval.

Although not impossible, federal clemency is even more complex, time-consuming, expensive, and harder to get than state clemency. For example, as of July 13, 2015, President Barack Obama has approved only 64 pardons in six-and-a-half years.

Second, though this man made one mistake under tremendous peer and financial pressure against his better judgment, he almost immediately tried to fix the situation.

Unfortunately, it was too late. In addition to committing a very serious crime, and putting his and his family's life at risk, he violated his law enforcement oath and disappointed his family, friends, neighbors and fellow community members.

Third, he was a model inmate. He helped other inmates develop a strong faith and learn work skills.

Finally, when he left prison he did *everything right*, and certainly influenced others to lead crime-free and productive lives.

Again, a good and fair result where a felon earned a second chance.

CHAPTER SEVEN

GETTING STATE LICENSES EVEN *WITHOUT* RESTORATION OF CIVIL RIGHTS

Voting and serving on a jury are important civic duties. While clemency will allow felons to regain these civil rights, most felons want clemency RCR because it will help them get a state license, better paying jobs, and more business opportunities.

In 2011, the Legislature passed a bill to "de-couple" state licenses from RCR unless the felony conviction (or first-degree misdemeanor conviction) is "directly related" to the desired license.

Ch. 2011-207, L.O.F. (CS/SB 146) by Senator Chris Smith (D-Ft. Lauderdale) and Rep. Dwayne Taylor (D-Daytona Beach) provides, in part, "a state agency may not deny an application for a license, permit, certificate, or employment based on the applicant's lack of civil rights."

The law doesn't apply to a concealed weapon or firearm. Without this change in the law, most felons are denied state licenses if their crimes involve "moral turpitude," or another common law, or a specific statutory disqualifier.

The key is how state agencies implement this law (which is named after the late Senate President Jim King of Jacksonville to help felons "get to work").

As discussed in Chapter 13, inmates need lots of help after jail or prison to reenter the community. Of course, the most important factor to not reoffending is for the former inmate to get a job and

51

become a productive member of society, which is easier said than done.

In a competitive job market, convicted felons will always be up against other applicants who, at first look, are more qualified and not a risk to hire.

This good 2011 law, passed with strong bipartisan support and approved by Governor Rick Scott, strikes a balance to help most felons get a shot at a state license, job and second chance.

By way of example, below are 29 state licenses required by the Florida Legislature and issued by the Florida Department of Business and Professional Regulation. While each has certain specific criteria and regulatory requirements, the 2011 "decoupling law" hopefully will benefit applicants who seek these licenses.

- Alcoholic Beverages and Tobacco
- Architects
- Asbestos Contractors and Consultants
- Athlete Agents
- Auctioneers
- Barbers
- Boxing, Kickboxing and Mixed Martial Arts
- Building Code Administrators and Inspectors
- Certified Public Accounting
- Community Association Managers
- Construction Industry
- Cosmetology
- Drugs, Devices and Cosmetics Program
- Electrical and Alarm Contractors

- Elevators and Other Conveyances, Technicians, Inspectors and Companies

- Employee Leasing Companies

- Geologists

- Harbor Pilots

- Home Inspectors

- Hotels, Motels, Apartments and other lodging

- Interior Design

- Landscape Architecture

- Mold-Related Services

- Pari-Mutuel Wagering Facilities

- Real Estate

- Restaurants, Take-outs, Delivery, Caterers, and Mobile Food Vendors

- Talent Agencies

- Veterinary Medicine

- Yacht and Ship Brokers, and Salespersons

Other state agencies grant insurance, financial, health-related, education and other specialized licenses. Time will tell how state agencies implement this law, and how it will be interpreted by the administrative and appellate courts.

CHAPTER EIGHT

OTHER TYPES OF EXECUTIVE CLEMENCY

While this book discusses the most common types of executive clemency, there are two other types called "Remission of Fines and Forfeitures" and "Restoration of Alien Status Under Florida Law." Both of these types are rarely granted.

Rule 4.I. states:

The Governor has the unfettered discretion to deny clemency at any time, for any reason. The Governor, with the approval of at least two members of the Clemency Board, has the unfettered discretion to grant, at any time, for any reason, the following forms of clemency:

E. Remission of Fines and Forfeitures

A Remission of Fines or Forfeitures suspends, reduces, or removes fines or forfeitures.

None of these were approved during Governor Scott's first term (2011-2015).

Rule 4.I.H. states:

H. Restoration of Alien Status under Florida Law

The Restoration of Alien Status Under Florida Law restores to an applicant who is not a citizen of the United States such rights enjoyed by him or her, under the authority of the State of Florida, which were lost as a result of a conviction of any crime that is a felony or would be a felony under Florida law, except the specific authority to own, possess, or use firearms. However, restoration of these rights shall not affect the immigration status of the applicant (i.e., a certificate evidencing Restoration of Alien Status Under Florida Law shall not be a ground for relief from removal proceedings initiated by the United States Immigration and Naturalization Service).

Note: *The Immigration and Naturalization Service (INS) is now called Immigration and Customs Enforcement (ICE), and is part of the U.S. Department of Homeland Security.*

One of these was approved between 2011 and 2014.

Rule 5.C. states:

5. Eligibility

C. Remission of Fines and Forfeitures

A person may not apply for a remission of fines and forfeitures unless he or she has completed all sentences imposed and all conditions of supervision have expired or been completed, including, but not limited to, parole, probation, community control, control release, and conditional release.

CHAPTER NINE

IMMIGRATION AND EXECUTIVE CLEMENCY

Chapter Four discussed pardons, and the many reasons why obtaining this type of clemency can be helpful. Other reasons are to help certain non-U.S. citizens avoid deportation, and to maybe extend their work visas, which is a specialized and technical area of federal law. (As with other aspects of this book, you should consult legal counsel to determine how certain convictions are treated.)

Pardons generally do not affect an individual's immigration status. However, in some limited circumstances, a pardon from particular crimes can: (1) protect against removal from the United States, and (2) allow a person who is not admissible to the United States because of a conviction to enter the United States.

Full and Unconditional Pardons

For the purposes of immigration law, a pardon must be full and unconditional to create a waiver for a conviction.[17] If the conviction arose under federal law, the President must issue the pardon. If the conviction arose under the laws of a state, the governor of that state must issue the pardon. Pardons from foreign governments do not create the same immigration benefits.

The pardon can't have any limitations or conditions, nor can it be automatically issued by operation of state statute. For example, the pardon can't withhold the right to carry a firearm, the right to vote, or any other civil right. Similarly, it can't be conditioned upon

---

[17] INA § 237(a)(2)(A)(vi).

any event, such as completion of the term of incarceration or probation.

A Pardon Can Protect Against Removal from the United States

For the purposes of immigration law, a pardon does not eliminate a conviction. Rather, a pardon creates an automatic "waiver of removability" for certain crimes that are specifically listed in a particular section of the immigration statutes.

These crimes include crimes involving moral turpitude (an immigration term covering many serious crimes), aggravated felonies (another immigration term covering many serious crimes), and convictions for high-speed flight from an immigration check point.[18]

Simply put, if you obtain a pardon for certain types of convictions, the government can't remove you from the United States based solely on those convictions.

Because the list of convictions is limited, even a pardon doesn't protect against being removed from the United States for individuals who've been convicted of many crimes including domestic violence, firearm offenses, or controlled substance offenses.

Along these lines, the pardon must cover every prior conviction that the government identifies as a basis for removal. For example, if an individual receives a pardon for multiple convictions, the pardon may protect against deportation based on some of these convictions, but not others. In this circumstance, the government can still remove the individual from the United States, because the pardon doesn't cover all of the person's prior convictions.

Similarly, the immigration law lists some crimes in multiple categories. For instance, trafficking in firearms is an aggravated

---

[18] INA § 237(a)(2)A)(vi).

felony and a firearms offense. In this instance, a pardon can't stop removal because it's ineffective against a firearms offense.[19]

A Pardon's Effect on Gaining Admission to the United States

Under immigration law, the question of whether a person is "admissible" arises when: (1) a non-citizen seeks to enter the United States; (2) an individual is physically present in the United States without being "admitted" or "paroled," (i.e., a person can enter the United States unlawfully, or be held at a border before being immigration officials formally allow him enter); or (3) an individual applies for an adjustment of his immigration status (such as applying to become a lawful permanent resident).[20]

A person can become "inadmissible" because of certain convictions.

Some federal courts have ruled that a pardon does not apply to a person who's deemed inadmissible to the United States. At the same time, the U.S. State Department (which is responsible for processing visas at overseas U.S. consulates) has waived "inadmissibility" for individuals who have full and unconditional pardons related to convictions of crimes involving moral turpitude and other criminal offenses.[21]

Media and Political Candidates' Attention to Immigration Issues

In summer 2015, immigration, and how the criminal justice system deals with illegal aliens and certain criminals, became the focus of national news:

- On June 16, 2015, presidential candidate Donald Trump made controversial references to some Mexican immigrants as rapists and criminals during his campaign announcement speech in New York City. His exact quote was:

---

[19] INA § 237(a)(2)(A)(i)-(iv).
[20] Matter of Suh, 23 I&N Dec. 626 (BIA 2003).
[21] INA § 212 (a).

"When Mexico sends its people, they're not sending their best. They're not sending you. They're sending people that have lots of problems, and they're bringing those problems with us. They're bringing drugs. They're bringing crime. They're rapists. And some, I assume, are good people."

The controversy pushed immigration issues to the forefront of the 2016 presidential campaign as most candidates in both parties and the media responded to Mr. Trump's declaration.

- On July 1, 2015, a repeat felon named Juan Francisco Lopez-Sanchez was accused of killing Kathryn Steinle, a 32 year-old woman who was walking with her father in San Francisco's Embarcadero waterfront area. The alleged killer had been deported *five times* to Mexico, but was back in California based on San Francisco's lenient "sanctuary city" status that provides protections to certain immigrants. The defendant was released from a city jail for an old marijuana case without federal officials being notified he was clearly deportable.

- On July 23, 2015, as outrage mounted over this murder, the U.S. House of Representatives passed legislation called "Kate's Law" (named after the deceased Ms. Steinle) by a vote of 241 to 179 to prevent the U.S. Department of Justice from providing federal grants to cities and counties that offer protections to certain immigrants living illegally in the U.S.

Regardless of who is elected president and to Congress -- starting in January 2017 -- immigration reform will likely be a top priority. Any new federal law almost certainly will include mandatory deportations for certain crimes.

CHAPTER TEN

CRIME VICTIMS' RIGHTS

Section 960.03 (14) of Florida Law Defines a Crime Victim As:

(a) A person who suffers personal physical injury or death as a direct result of a crime;

(b) A person younger than 18 years of age who was present at the scene of a crime, saw or heard the crime, and suffered a psychiatric or psychological injury because of the crime, but who was not physically injured; or

(c) A person against whom a forcible felony was committed, and who suffers a psychiatric or psychological injury as a direct result of that crime but who does not otherwise sustain a personal physical injury or death.

Victims Are Always Consulted

In Executive Clemency cases, the crime victims are always consulted by the FCOR's Victim Advocate and given an opportunity to appear at the clemency hearing, or to write a letter stating if they oppose or support the clemency.

A victim's or family member's position is given great weight, especially in the most serious crimes with deaths or injuries. The state attorney who prosecuted the case also is contacted and usually provides a recommendation. When the victim is opposed to clemency, the state attorney almost always follows their lead and also opposes the clemency.

Florida's elected state attorneys prosecute cases in 20 judicial circuits. Based on population, the larger judicial circuits are comprised of only one county, while multiple smaller counties comprise other judicial circuits. For example, the 13th Judicial Circuit includes only Hillsborough County, while the 2nd Judicial Circuit is comprised of six counties: Franklin, Gadsden, Jefferson, Leon, Liberty and Wakulla.

The victim's and prosecutor's positions are very important. Any opposition makes obtaining clemency even harder, though not impossible.

Article I, Section 16(b) of the Florida Constitution, states:

Rights of accused and of victims.

(b) Victims of crime or their lawful representatives, including the next of kin of homicide victims, are entitled to the right to be informed, to be present, and to be heard when relevant, at all crucial stages of criminal proceedings, to the extent that these rights do not interfere with the constitutional rights of the accused.

Florida law § 960.001, entitled "**Guidelines for fair treatment of victims and witnesses in the criminal justice and juvenile justice systems**" states, in part:

(1)(a) Information concerning services available to victims of adult and juvenile crime.

As provided in s. 27.0065, state attorneys and public defenders shall gather information regarding the following services in the geographic boundaries of their respective circuits, and shall provide such information to each law enforcement agency with jurisdiction within such geographic boundaries. Law enforcement personnel shall ensure, through distribution of a victim's rights information card or brochure at the crime scene, during the criminal investigation, and in any other appropriate manner, that victims are given, as a matter of course at the earliest possible time, information about:

Second Chances

1. The availability of crime victim compensation, if applicable;

2. Crisis intervention services, supportive or bereavement counseling, social service support referrals, and community-based victim treatment programs;

3. The role of the victim in the criminal or juvenile justice process, including what the victim may expect from the system as well as what the system expects from the victim;

4. The stages in the criminal or juvenile justice process which are of significance to the victim and the manner in which information about such stages can be obtained;

5. The right of a victim, who is not incarcerated, including the victim's parent or guardian if the victim is a minor, the lawful representative of the victim or of the victim's parent or guardian if the victim is a minor, and the next of kin of a homicide victim, to be informed, to be present, and to be heard when relevant, at all crucial stages of a criminal or juvenile proceeding, to the extent that this right does not interfere with constitutional rights of the accused, as provided by s. 16(b), Art. I of the State Constitution;

6. In the case of incarcerated victims, the right to be informed and to submit written statements at all crucial stages of the criminal proceedings, parole proceedings, or juvenile proceedings; and

7. The right of a victim to a prompt and timely disposition of the case in order to minimize the period during which the victim must endure the responsibilities and stress involved to the extent that this right does not interfere with the constitutional rights of the accused.

(b) Information for purposes of notifying victim or appropriate next of kin of victim or other designated contact of victim.

(c) Information concerning protection available to victim or witness.

(d) Notification of scheduling changes.

(e) Advance notification to victim or relative of victim concerning judicial proceedings; right to be present.

(f) Information concerning release from incarceration from a county jail, municipal jail, juvenile detention facility, or residential commitment facility.

(g) Consultation with victim or guardian or family of victim.

(h) Return of property to victim.

(i) Notification to employer and explanation to creditors of victim or witness.

(j) Notification of right to request restitution.

(k) Notification of right to submit impact statement.

(l) Local witness coordination services.

(m) Victim assistance education and training.

(n) General victim assistance.

(o) Victim's rights information card or brochure.

(p) Information concerning escape from a state correctional institution, county jail, juvenile detention facility, or residential commitment facility.

(q) Presence of victim advocate during discovery deposition; testimony of victim of a sexual offense.

(r) Implementing crime prevention in order to protect the safety of persons and property, as prescribed in the State Comprehensive Plan.

(s) Attendance of victim at same school as defendant.

(t) Use of a polygraph examination or other truth-telling device with victim.

(u) Presence of victim advocates during forensic medical examination.

Most Orders of Judgment and Sentence in criminal cases include a special condition whereby the defendant will have "no contact" with the victim. Yet, in clemency cases a frequent question is "has the applicant apologized to the victim?"

If there is heartfelt remorse, the only practical way to do this is to send an apology letter to the victim through the state attorney's office. Clemency applicants should not attempt to contact the victim directly by phone, email, text, letter or in person.

Please see Appendix E for the complete text of Florida Law 960.001: Guidelines for fair treatment of victims and witnesses in the criminal justice and juvenile justice systems.

CHAPTER ELEVEN

CONTACT THE DECISION-MAKERS: WHO AND HOW?

Governor and Florida Cabinet
(aka: The Board of Executive Clemency)

Office of Executive Clemency

Since many clemency applicants can't afford a lawyer, Chapters 11 and 12 describe who to contact and how to contact them. Clemency applicants can write letters and appear at the hearing, and family members and other advocates can support the applicant with character letters and testimony at the hearing.

Under Florida law, all correspondence sent to the Governor's Office, which is not exempt or confidential pursuant to Chapter 119 of the Florida Statutes, is a public record. All public record electronic mail sent through this website will be posted to Project Sunburst at http://www.flgov.com/sunburst and will be accessible to the public.

If you don't want the public record contents of your email or your email address to be published on this website -- or to be provided to the public in response to a public records request -- *do not* send electronic mail to this entity.

Be aware that any personal information sent in correspondence, such as home addresses and telephone numbers, may be posted to the Sunburst public records website.

All written information should be sent directly to:

The Office of Executive Clemency
Julia McCall, Coordinator
4070 Esplanade Way
Tallahassee, FL 32399-2450

Toll Free: 1-800-435-8286
Phone: (850) 488-2952
Fax: (850) 488-0695
Email: Clemencyweb@fpc.state.fl.us
Website: https://www.fcor.state.fl.us/clemency.shtml

Florida Clemency Rule 16 governs confidentiality of information presented to the Board:

Florida Clemency Rule 16.

Confidentiality of Records and Documents:

Due to the nature of the information presented to the Clemency Board, all records and documents generated and gathered in the clemency process as set forth in the Rules of Executive Clemency are confidential, and shall not be made available for inspection to any person except members of the Clemency Board and their staff. Only the governor, and no other member of the Clemency Board, nor any other state entity that may be in the possession of Clemency Board materials, has the discretion to allow such records and documents to be inspected or copied. Access to such materials, as approved by the governor, does not constitute a waiver of confidentiality.

Governor Rick Scott

Executive Office of Governor Rick Scott
400 S. Monroe Street Street
Tallahassee, FL 32399
(850) 488-7146

Email: RickScott@eog.myflorida.com

Website: http://www.flgov.com/

Governor Richard L. Scott

Rick Scott is the 45th Governor of the great State of Florida. As promised during his campaign, Scott is focused on creating jobs and turning Florida's economy around.

Born in Bloomington, Illinois, and raised in Kansas City, Missouri, his father was in the 82nd Airborne during World War II. After the war, Gov. Scott's father was a city bus driver and then a truck driver. His mother worked as a J.C. Penney clerk. At times the family struggled financially, and when Gov. Scott started public school, they lived in public housing.

In high school, Gov. Scott met Ann, and the high school sweethearts have been married for 43 years and have two married daughters, Allison and Jordan, and three grandsons, Auguste, Quinton and Sebastian.

After attending high school and community college, Gov. Scott enlisted in the United States Navy, where he served on active duty aboard the USS Glover as a radar man. The G.I. Bill enabled Gov. Scott to attend college and law school.

While enrolled at the University of Missouri-Kansas City and working full-time at a local grocery store, Gov. Scott and Ann made their first significant foray into the business world by buying two Kansas City doughnut shops for Gov. Scott's mother to manage. Following graduation from UMKC with a degree in business administration, Gov. Scott earned a law degree from Southern Methodist University. After law school, Gov. Scott stayed in Dallas, working for the city's largest law firm, Johnson & Swanson, primarily representing companies in the health care, oil and gas and communication industries.

In 1987, while still practicing law, Gov. Scott made an offer to purchase HCA, Inc. When the offer was rejected, Gov. Scott started Columbia Hospital Corporation with his and Ann's entire life savings of $125,000. Gov. Scott also started Conservatives for Patient's Rights, which advocated for free market principles of choice, competition, accountability and personal responsibility in health care. Gov. Scott wanted to prevent further government encroachment on the rights of patients.

When Gov. Scott left Columbia in 1997 at age 44, it was one of the most admired companies in America. It had grown to become the world's largest health care company with more than 340 hospitals, 135 surgery centers, and 550 home health locations in 37 states and two foreign countries. Columbia employed more than 285,000 people, making it the 7th largest U.S. employer and the 12th largest employer worldwide.

Faith, Family and Community

Before moving to Tallahassee, the Scott family lived in Naples. When they are back home, they still attend Naples Community Church, which Rick and Ann helped start in 2006.

Throughout their lives, Gov. Scott and First Lady Ann have served their community through volunteer and charitable work. Rick has served on the National Board of the United Way, and Gov. Scott and Ann have worked with World Vision to create a primary health care system in Bunyala, a poor area of Kenya. In addition, they fund scholarships that enable a low-income student to attend SMU Law School each year. They also fund an entrepreneur contest at George Washington University where one of their daughters received a business degree.

Businessman and Entrepreneur

Gov. Scott is known as an innovator in business, health care, and politics. His specialization was in health care mergers and acquisitions, and it was during his work on these transactions that he recognized how patients could be better served by improving hospital efficiency, lowering costs, and focusing on better outcomes.

Through his entrepreneurship, Gov. Scott developed a reputation in the health care industry for providing affordable, high quality care to patients. As Governor, he brings a similar vision for quality and efficiency to benefit the people of Florida.

Attorney General Pam Bondi

Office of Attorney General
State of Florida
The Capitol PL-01
Tallahassee, FL 32399-1050
(850) 414-3300

Email: Pam.Bondi@myfloridalegal.com
Website: http://www.myfloridalegal.com/

Attorney General Pam Bondi

A native of Tampa, Pam Bondi became Florida's 37th Attorney General after being elected on November 2, 2010. Attorney General Bondi was sworn in to office January 4, 2011.

Attorney General Bondi is focused on protecting Floridians and upholding Florida's laws and the Constitution. Some of her top priorities are: defending Florida's constitutional rights against the federal health care law; strengthening penalties to stop pill mills; aggressively investigating mortgage fraud and Medicaid fraud; and ensuring Florida is compensated for Deepwater Horizon oil spill losses.

Transparency and openness in government have been important throughout her career, and Attorney General Bondi continues to support Florida's Sunshine laws.

Attorney General Bondi is dedicated to serving her community, including her membership on the Board of The Spring, Tampa's domestic violence shelter. In her role as Attorney General, she serves on the Special Olympics Florida Board of Directors and is proud to promote their mission of assisting people with disabilities with being productive and respected members of our communities.

National Association of Drug Diversion Investigators recognized Attorney General Bondi with 2011 Leadership Award for her efforts to stop prescription drug abuse. In addition, Attorney General Bondi was awarded a special recognition by the Florida Police Chiefs Association for "efforts to reduce prescription drug abuse and strengthen Florida's Prescription Drug Monitoring Program through additional legislation via the 'pill mill' bill." Additionally, Attorney General Bondi was awarded the Florida Board of Medicine Chairman's Recognition Award for her dedication and service to the people of Florida for her efforts to fight prescription drug abuse.

Attorney General Bondi was awarded the Distinguished Alumna Award in 2011 by Stetson University for extraordinary service to Stetson Law and to the legal profession. During her career as a prosecutor, Attorney General Bondi was awarded the Lawyers of Distinction Award by the Tampa Bay Review for outstanding performance.

Attorney General Bondi is a graduate of University of Florida and Stetson Law School and has served as a prosecutor for more than 18 years. As an assistant state attorney for the 13th judicial district, her investigative and courtroom experience includes the successful prosecution of numerous first-degree murder cases and two capital cases.

Chief Financial Officer Jeff Atwater

Office Location:
Office of the Chief Financial Officer
Plaza Level 11, The Capitol
Tallahassee, Florida 32399
(850) 413-3100

Mailing:
Office of the Chief Financial Officer
Florida Department of Financial Services
200 East Gaines Street
Tallahassee, FL 32399-0301

Email: Jeff.Atwater@MyFloridaCFO.com
Website: http://www.myfloridacfo.com

Jeff Atwater, Chief Financial Officer

Jeff Atwater serves the citizens of the state of Florida as the state's elected Chief Financial Officer, State Fire Marshal, and as a member of the Florida Cabinet.

A fifth-generation Floridian, husband and father of four, Jeff Atwater was elected Florida's Chief Financial Officer on November 2, 2010, and sworn into office on January 4, 2011. He was reelected to a second term on November 4, 2014, and sworn into office on January 6, 2015. His commitment to public service began in 1993, when his hometown of North Palm Beach elected him Vice Mayor. Mr. Atwater was subsequently elected to the House of Representatives in 2000 and the Florida Senate in 2002 and was unanimously selected by his fellow senators to serve as Senate President in 2008.

Jeff Atwater's family has had a long and distinguished commitment to public service at local, municipal and state levels. Family values of fairness, stewardship of the public trust, and an unshakeable faith in the American ethos have informed his sense of duty and responsibility in all facets of his public and private careers.

He believes that the principal role of government is to create the conditions where the individuals, families and businesses of Florida are given every opportunity to flourish. Hard work, the value of education, commitment to Judeo-Christian ethics, and belief in the promise of America are to be encouraged and rewarded, not stymied by an overreaching government.

CFO Atwater's priorities since assuming office have been to aggressively eliminate the fraud that increases the cost of living for Floridians, reduce regulations that inhibit job growth and economic expansion, expand his earlier efforts at fiscal transparency and governmental accountability, and protect the state's most vulnerable citizens from financial harm and abuse.

Mr. Atwater earned his bachelor's degree in finance and an MBA from the University of Florida. His private sector experiences, which included twenty-five years of community banking, provide him a unique and valuable perspective on the sacrifices and challenges facing the business men and women of Florida, as well as the impact of government on the individuals and families of this state. In addition to his service as an elected official, CFO Atwater has performed volunteer work with many charitable and not-for-profit organizations and has served on a number of governing boards, including the United Way, Chamber of Commerce, Big Brothers and Big Sisters, and Take Stock in Children, among others.

Commissioner of Agriculture Adam H. Putnam

Florida Department of Agriculture and Consumer Services
Plaza Level 10, the Capitol
400 S. Monroe St.
Tallahassee, FL 32399-0800
1-800 HELP-FLA or 1-800-435-7352

Email: Adam.Putnam@FreshFromFlorida.com

Website: http://www.freshfromflorida.com/

Adam H. Putnam, Commissioner of Agriculture and Consumer Services

Adam Putnam was elected to serve a second term as Florida's Commissioner of Agriculture on November 4, 2014, and was sworn into office on January 6, 2015. In this capacity, he oversees the Florida Department of Agriculture and Consumer Services and serves as a member of Florida's Cabinet.

Commissioner Putnam's priorities include fostering the growth and diversification of Florida agriculture; expanding access to Florida's abundance of fresh produce, seafood and other products; securing a stable, reliable and diverse supply of energy; protecting the quantity and quality of the state's water supply; and safeguarding consumers from deceptive business practices.

Commissioner Putnam is also focused on creating opportunities for our nation's wounded veterans to hunt, fish and participate in other outdoor activities on Florida's public lands. More than 300 veterans have enjoyed recreational opportunities on Florida State Forests through Operation Outdoor Freedom, a program of the Florida Forest Service he established in 2011.

Previously, Commissioner Putnam served five terms as Congressman for Florida's 12th Congressional District in the U.S. House of Representatives. He was recognized as a leader on a variety of issues, including water, energy and government transparency and efficiency. Commission Putnam was acknowledged for his efforts to bring comprehensive restoration to the Everglades, reform food safety laws, modernize programs to ensure Florida agriculture remains a leader throughout the nation and increase access to fresh fruits and vegetables to counter childhood obesity.

While in Congress, Commissioner Putnam was elected by his peers to serve as the Republican Policy Chairman during the 109th Congress and Chairman of the House Republican Conference for the 110th Congress, the highest elected leadership position any Floridian of either party has held in

Washington. Commissioner Putnam also served as a member of the House Committees on Government Reform, Agriculture, Rules and Financial Services.

Before he was elected to Congress, Commissioner Putnam served in the Florida House of Representatives from 1996 to 2000. He graduated from the University of Florida with a Bachelor of Science in Food and Resource Economics.

Commissioner Putnam is a fifth generation Floridian who grew up in the citrus and cattle industry. He and his wife, Melissa, have four children.

CHAPTER TWELVE

CONTACT THE DECISION-MAKERS: WHO AND HOW?

Florida Commission on Offender Review

4070 Esplanade Way
Tallahassee, FL 32399-2450
Attn: Commission Clerk
Toll Free (855) 850-8196 ... or (850) 487-3259
FAX: (850) 921-8712

In addition to directly making parole decisions, the Commission investigates all clemency cases and makes an "advisory" recommendation to the Board of Executive Clemency.

Florida Crime Victims' Bill of Rights
Florida Constitutional Amendment, Article I

Victims of crime or their lawful representatives, including the next of kin of homicide victims, are entitled to be informed, present, and heard, when relevant, at all crucial stages of criminal proceedings, to the extent that these rights do not interfere with the constitutional rights of the accused.

Florida Commission on Offender Review
(formerly Florida Parole Commission)

COMMISSIONER BIOGRAPHIES

Commissioner Tena M. Pate, Chair initiated her career in criminal justice in 1979 with the Office of State Attorney for the First Judicial Circuit, and later became the first person appointed to serve as Victims' Advocate for Okaloosa and Walton Counties.

Commissioner Pate relocated to Tallahassee in 1989 to accept a position in the Executive Office of the Governor. In 1993, she accepted the appointment as Florida's Victims' Rights Coordinator in the administration of Governor Lawton Chiles.

While in the Governor's Office, she also served as a Clemency Assistant and State Attorney Liaison. She served in this capacity for three governors until her appointment to the Florida Parole Commission. Commissioner Pate was initially appointed to the Commission in 2003 by Governor Bush to fill a Commission vacancy.

On June 24, 2004, Commissioner Pate was appointed to a full six-year term ending June 2010. In 2010 and 2011, Commissioner Pate was reappointed by Governors Crist and Scott and the Florida Cabinet for a full six-year term ending June 30, 2016. On August 19, 2014, she was re-appointed to serve her third two-year term as Chair by Governor Rick Scott and members of the Cabinet.

Commissioner Pate has over 30 years of experience working in criminal justice and government relations and is a member of the Association of Paroling Authorities, Florida Council on Crime and

Delinquency, Florida Police Chiefs Association, Leadership Florida and a graduate of the Florida Department of Law Enforcement Chief Executive Seminar.

* * * * * * *

Commissioner Melinda N. Coonrod, Vice Chair began her criminal justice career in 1992 when she was appointed to serve as an Assistant State Attorney for the Second Judicial Circuit.

As a prosecutor with the State Attorney's Office, Commissioner Coonrod handled a diverse set of criminal cases. She was the lead prosecutor in more than 57 jury trials and more than 30 non-jury trials.

During her career as a prosecutor, Commissioner Coonrod gained extensive criminal law experience, and became well-versed in the Florida criminal justice system. She prosecuted perpetrators of crimes, advocated sentencing of those found guilty and worked closely with victims and various law enforcement agencies.

Commissioner Coonrod later served as an Administrative Hearing Officer with the Florida Department of Agriculture and Consumer Services Division of Licensing where she presided over 1400 hearings involving the denial, suspension and revocation of licensure under Chapters 493 and 790, Florida Statutes.

Her experience also includes representing children before the courts as a certified court -appointed Guardian Ad Litem, providing training seminars to various law enforcement agencies, and teaching graduate and undergraduate courses as an adjunct instructor at Florida State University College of Criminology and Criminal Justice.

On June 26, 2012, Commissioner Coonrod was appointed by the Governor and Cabinet to serve on the Commission. On April 29, 2013, she was unanimously confirmed by the Florida Senate to serve a six-year term, which expires June 30, 2018.

On September 19, 2014, the Governor and Cabinet appointed Commissioner Coonrod to serve a two-year term as Vice Chair of the Commission.

* * * * * * *

Commissioner Richard D. Davison, Secretary began his criminal justice career in 1989 as an Assistant State Attorney in the Ninth Judicial Circuit where he prosecuted juvenile delinquency, misdemeanor, and traffic cases in jury and nonjury trials.

In 1991, he became the staff attorney for the Florida House of Representatives Committee on Criminal Justice. He then served as an Assistant Statewide Prosecutor for Florida's Office of Statewide Prosecution where he prosecuted white-collar crime, organized crime and other criminal enterprises.

Following the creation of the Florida Department of Juvenile Justice in 1994, Commission Davison served as that Department's Director of Legislative Affairs, Assistant General Counsel, and Deputy Secretary. Subsequently, Commissioner Davison was appointed Deputy Secretary of the Florida Department of Corrections.

Prior to his appointment to the Commission, Davison served as Legal Counsel and Director of Administration for the Gadsden County Sheriff's Office as well as program coordinator for the City of Tallahassee Community Corrections Restorative Justice Program.

Commissioner Davison received a Bachelor of Science degree from Florida State University in 1984 and a Doctor of Jurisprudence from the University of Florida in 1988.

Commissioner Davison was appointed by Governor Scott and the Cabinet on August 19, 2014 and was confirmed by the Florida Senate on April 29, 2015 to serve a six-year term, which extends until June 30, 2020.

CHAPTER THIRTEEN

TRANSITION AND RE-ENTRY AFTER PRISON OR JAIL

Florida has nearly 101,000 inmates in 56 state prisons. State prison inmates are 93% male and 7% female. Eighty percent eventually will leave, and one-third will be released at their "end-of-sentence" during the next 12 months.

Thousands more prisoners are released annually from Florida's 67 county jails after completing sentences of one year or less, and from ten federal prisons in the state.

As citizens who want safe communities and taxpayers who pay the bills, we all have a vested interest in these issues:

- Where will the former inmate live?
- Who will provide them with clothes, transportation and food?
- How will they get a state identification card or driver's license?
- Where will they get alcohol and/or drug treatment, rehabilitation, redirection and counseling?
- Who will pay for it?
- Can they get a job and if so, where?
- Will work force education and training be available in their community?
- Will they commit new crimes?

FDOC data based on 2009 releases shows 26% of released Florida inmates will commit new crimes and return to state prison within three (3) years. More recent data from the Smart Justice Alliance Florida indicates 43% of new admissions are reoffenders. Some released convicted felons know no other life, and will commit new crimes. It's just a matter of if and when they get caught.

Many released non-violent inmates will not reoffend, as they have a new way of thinking and acting. They're not going back to prison, but likely will need help from family, community stakeholders and government programs to transition back to being productive law-abiding citizens.

Then there are the thousands "in the middle" that could go either way: back to a life of crime or onto a self-sufficient and productive life. These former inmates will need the most help, especially upon release and in the short term.

The Florida Department of Corrections' role in public safety extends beyond the walls and fences of its prisons. Its role is to use the time inmates are in its "care, custody and control" to prepare them to be law-abiding citizens once they're released. The FDOC meets this obligation by offering inmates opportunities to improve their educational levels, job and life skills while serving their sentences. Then once released, they will become a contributing factor in a community's safety and its economy.

FDOC's Re-entry Centers
The FDOC is laser-focused on increasing and improving re-entry programs. The FDOC has numerous education, work, training and self-improvement courses at most prisons.

With the goal of successful transitions back into communities, plus to reduce recidivism, the FDOC and private contractors operate six designated re-entry centers:

1. Baker Re-Entry Center (under the direction of Baker Correctional Institution, in North Florida west of Jacksonville), serving inmates releasing to Northeast Florida.

2. Gadsden Re-Entry Center (in North Florida, west of Tallahassee), serving inmates releasing to the Panhandle counties.

3. Everglades Re-Entry Center (under the direction of Everglades Correctional Institution, in South Florida), serving inmates releasing to Miami-Dade County.

4. Sago Palm Re-Entry Center (in western Palm Beach County).

5. Polk Correctional Re-Entry Institution (Central Florida, serving inmates releasing to Hillsborough, Pinellas and Polk counties).

6. Baker Correctional Re-Entry Institution (in North Florida, serving inmates releasing to Duval County).

These prisons partner with local law enforcement agencies and nonprofits, utilize state and federal grants, and work with re-entry portals to help soon-to-be-released inmates be ready to work and succeed in their new life.[22]

FDOC's New Goal of "Transformative Rehabilitation"

Policymakers and corrections officials in Florida and around the country are focusing on how to improve public safety, lower the cost of incarceration, reduce recidivism, and rehabilitate inmates (while they're a captive audience).

FDOC Secretary Julie Jones (one of the most-respected and effective managers in state government) described how the FDOC is trying to "embrace transformative rehabilitation" in a recent

---

[22] FDOC 2013-2016 Strategic Plan (pages 6-8)

media opinion editorial published by the *Sun-Sentinel*[23] in Ft. Lauderdale.

Secretary Jones described six (6) key strategies to:

- Engage inmates with programming and learning opportunities to help them succeed and prevent future crime.
- Shift the way Florida defines success in its institutional programming and community supervision and probation initiatives.
- Develop an individualized plan that addresses inmate's specific needs, ensuring their incarceration and supervision is a truly rehabilitative process.
- Implement institutional programs ranging from substance abuse treatment and counseling to educational and vocational classes that are essential to keeping an inmate on the right track, and ensuring their incarceration creates positive change in their lives.
- Provide inmates with an opportunity to leave the facilities with the skills, certifications and education needed to help them successfully reintegrate into communities is critical to reducing the rate at which offenders reengage in criminal behavior.
- Utilize FDOC's numerous probation offices to help felons who have probation instead of, or after, state prison.

The FDOC's goal is to provide inmates with the proper guidance and support to ensure that they walk out of Florida's prisons prepared to overcome hurdles that previously may have contributed to them committing a crime.

---

[23] Julie Jones, Florida Department of Corrections embraces transformative rehabilitation, Sun-Sentinel (June 8, 2015), http://www.sun-sentinel.com/opinion/commentary/fl-viewpoint-rehab-20150608-story.html

Transition from Prison to Community Initiative (TPCI)

Created in 1993 and updated in 2009, the National Institute of Corrections (NIC) has developed a comprehensive model for the transition process. Fourteen states have adopted this model. The key elements are:

- Mobilize interdisciplinary, collaborative leadership teams convened by corrections agencies to guide re-entry efforts at state and local levels.

- Engage in a rational planning process to carefully define goals, develop a clear understanding of reentering offender populations and their rates of recidivism, and review existing policies, procedures, and resources for re-entry.

- Integrate stages of offenders' processing through the justice/corrections system (beginning at commitment to prison or earlier and continuing through assessment, prison programming, preparation for release, release, and supervision in the community), resulting in a carefully planned process with close communication and collaboration among prison officials, releasing authorities, and post-prison supervision staff.

- Involve non-correctional stakeholders (public, private, and community agencies) who can provide services and support as re-entry efforts are planned and implemented.

- Assure that transitioning offenders are provided basic survival resources such as identification documents, housing, appropriate medications, linkages to community services and informal networks of support before, during, and after they are released from prison.

- Implement valid offender assessments at various stages of the offender's movement through the system.

- Target effective interventions, based on good research, to address the offender's risks and criminogenic needs identified by assessments.

- Expand the traditional roles of correctional staff beyond custody, security, accountability, and monitoring to include an integrated approach to offender management that engages offenders in the process of change.
- Develop the capacity to measure change toward specific outcomes and track information that can be used for planning future improvements.

Secretary Jones is engaging NIC in some elements of the FDOC model of Transformative Rehabilitation. FDOC will tailor some aspects of the NIC model to fit Florida's unique corrections environment.

P.R.I.D.E. = Rehabilitation*

The acronym PRIDE stands for "Prison Rehabilitative Industries and Diversified Enterprises, Inc." Although different than the formal re-entry programs, PRIDE has similar goals, and the two programs are not mutually exclusive.

Created in 1981 by the Florida Legislature as a private, not-for-profit inmate training program, in 2014 PRIDE trained 3,719 inmates in 42 diverse industries in 29 state correctional institutions.

PRIDE inmates worked almost 3.5 million hours, and trained in modern high-technology trades such as print and digital information, garments and apparel, furniture manufacturing, vehicle renovation, metal fabrication, dental and optical services.

With more than 30 years of experience, PRIDE's post-release track record is impressive: 63% of PRIDE-trained former inmates were placed in "relevant jobs and only 11% reoffended and returned to prison.[24] This successful national model was the brain child of drugstore owner and visionary Jack Eckerd.

---

[24] PRIDE Enterprises 2014 Annual Report, Prison Rehabilitative Industries and Diversified Enterprises, Inc.

*Disclosure: In 1994, the author was a federal lobbyist for PRIDE working on labor and compensation issues.

Special Re-entry Programs for Parole-Eligible Inmates

The FDOC also has transition and re-entry programs for inmates eligible for parole who are referred by the FCOR for "special programming." As parole was abolished for most crimes in 1983 and completely in 1995, only around 4,600 inmates are still eligible for parole.

These programs are utilized at these four prisons:

1. **Everglades C.I. in South Florida** has the "Correctional Transition Program" (also informally called the "FIU Program" because it was designed by faculty members from Florida International University).

2. **Sumter C.I. in Central Florida** has the Lifers Program.

3. **Wakulla C.I. in North Florida**, the first and largest faith-based male prison, has both the REEFS program (Realizing Educational, Emotional and Financial Smarts) and Celebrate Recovery programs.

4. **Charlotte C.I. in Southwest Florida** has the Life Path Program.

A CASE STUDY: The Big Bend AFTER Re-entry Coalition

There are 20 state prisons in North Florida and the Florida Panhandle within a several hour travel distance to Tallahassee. Every Florida community is different, and some more advanced than others. But most have community and faith-based transition and re-entry services available.

(2014),http://www.prideenterprises.org/Themes/PrideDefault/MediaContent/About/2014%20Annual%20Report/2014_Annual_Report.pdf

We know what works. For example, in my adopted hometown of Tallahassee (Florida's capital city), there's a group called Big Bend AFTER Re-entry Coalition (BBARC). "AFTER" is an acronym and goal statement for: "A Fight to End Recidivism."

The coalition members have access to lots of human capital: Tallahassee is the hub of state government, including the main office of the FDOC, and home to Florida State University (FSU), Florida Agricultural and Mechanical University (FAMU) and Tallahassee Community College (TCC).

FDOC and these colleges have hundreds of professionals and college professors who are experts in criminal justice issues and related fields. For example, many BBARC members are jail and corrections officials, or local, state and federal law enforcement officers and civilian workers.

The BBARC is a coalition of individuals and groups united to increase public safety and reduce recidivism through:

- Coordinating services in order to help inmates and formerly incarcerated people access identification documents, housing, education, employment, substance abuse intervention and mental health services.
- Educating the community about the benefits to community safety of assisting inmates and formerly incarcerated people in their transition.
- Collaborating with the Florida business community to increase employment opportunities for formerly incarcerated people.
- Providing information to employers and formerly incarcerated people about hiring incentives like the Work Opportunity Tax Credit and Federal Bonding insurance.

Similar citizen-driven reentry coalitions are at work in communities throughout the state. In Pensacola, REAP (Re-Entry Alliance of Pensacola) works with federal and state corrections systems to help returning citizens. In Miami-Dade, the South Florida Re-entry Task Force has opened the South Florida Re-entry Center Hub.

With around 3,000 inmates per month being released statewide, all Florida employers, community leaders, elected officials, faith leaders, and other taxpayers should do their part, no matter how large or small, to help an offender become a productive citizen.

CHAPTER FOURTEEN

RESENTENCING OF JUVENILE OFFENDERS IN POST-*GRAHAM* and *MILLER* CASES

This book has discussed Executive Clemency as a way to earn a second chance. Another type of second chance is the resentencing in Florida's trial courts of juveniles who committed serious, often violent, crimes before they were adults. Juvenile resentencing is one of the hottest policy and legal issues in criminal justice reform in Florida and around the country.

Why?

This policy debate intensified following the U.S. Supreme Court's landmark decision in *Graham v. State of Florida*, which involved Florida inmate Terrance Graham who at the age of 16 committed armed burglary and attempted robbery.[25] Under a plea agreement, a Florida trial court sentenced Graham to concurrent three-year terms (at the same time) of probation, and **withheld** adjudication of guilt.[26]

Graham's probation officer filed an affidavit with the trial court stating that Graham had violated his probation by committing other crimes.[27] The trial court adjudicated him guilty of the earlier charges, revoked his probation, and sentenced him to **life in prison for the burglary**.[28] This life sentence for a non-capital

---

[25] Graham v. Florida, 130 S. Ct. 2011, 2018 (U.S. 2010).
[26] Id.
[27] Id. at 2019.
[28] Id. at 2020.

felony gave him no possibility of release unless he was granted executive clemency.[29]

Graham challenged the constitutionality of his sentence under the Eighth Amendment's Cruel and Unusual Punishment Clause. The Florida First District Court of Appeal affirmed the trial court's decision, concluding his sentence was not disproportionate to the crime.[30] The Supreme Court of Florida denied review and the U.S. Supreme Court granted *certiorari* (a review of the lower court's decision).[31]

Writing the majority opinion, Associate Justice Anthony Kennedy (appointed by President Ronald Reagan in 1988) reaffirmed the idea that juvenile offenders are less deserving of the most severe punishments due to their lessened culpability.[32] The Court:

- Noted that it has been recognized that "defendants who do not kill, intend to kill, or foresee that life will be taken are categorically less deserving of the most serious forms of punishment than are murderers.[33]

- Concluded that juvenile offenders who did not kill or intend to kill have a twice-diminished moral culpability.[34]

- Found no justification for life without parole sentencing for juvenile non-homicide offenders through the four tenets of penological theory (retribution, deterrence, incapacitation, and rehabilitation).[35]

---

[29] § 921.002(1)(e), Fla. Stat. (2003).
[30] 982 So.2d 43, 53 (2008), rev'd, 130 S.Ct. 2011 (U.S. 2010).
[31] 990 So.2d 1058 (2008); 129 S.Ct. 2157 (2009).
[32] Graham, 130 S.Ct. at 2026 (quoting Roper v. Simmons, 543 U.S. 551, 556 (U.S. 2004)).
[33] Graham, 130 S.Ct. at 2026 (quoting Kennedy v. Louisiana, 554 U.S. 407, 415 (U.S. 2008)).
[34] Graham, 130 S.Ct. at 2027.
[35] Id. at 2029.

- Held that the imposition of life without parole sentences on a juvenile offender who did not commit homicide is prohibited by the Eighth Amendment.[36]

- Held that, while a state is not required to guarantee eventual freedom to a juvenile offender convicted of a non-homicide crime, it must give these types of offenders "*some meaningful opportunity to obtain release after demonstrated maturity and rehabilitation.*"[37]

In 2012, the U.S. Supreme Court heard *Miller v. Alabama* involving challenges brought by Alabama and Arkansas inmates who had each received life sentences without the possibility of parole following their convictions for capital felonies.[38] They had been tried as adults, despite the fact that they were both 14 years old when they committed their crimes.[39]

The trial courts imposed statutorily-mandated sentences of life imprisonment without the possibility of parole on each of the petitioners.[40] Both of the petitioner's challenged the constitution-ality of their sentences arguing that sentencing laws that mandate life in prison without parole for juvenile homicide offenders violated the Eighth Amendment.[41]

The Court reaffirmed the contrast between the culpability of juvenile offenders and the severity of a penalty, plus the diminished penological reasons for imposing the harshest sentences on juvenile offenders.[42]

The Court concluded that since the imposition of mandatory life-without-parole sentences on juvenile homicide offenders pre-

---

[36] Id. at 2034.
[37] Id. at 2028.
[38] Miller v. Alabama, 132 S.Ct. 2455, 2457 (U.S. 2012).
[39] Id.
[40] Id.
[41] Id.
[42] Id. at 2463.

cludes the judge from taking into account the offender's age and the characteristics attendant to it, the practice violates the principles of proportionality and is unconstitutional under the Eighth Amendment.[43]

The *Miller* precedent created a predicament in Florida where mandatory sentencing is in place for capital felonies. Effective in October, 1995, Florida law provided two sentencing options for persons convicted of a capital felony, death or life imprisonment without the possibility of parole.[44] This law requires that post-conviction proceedings be held to determine if the defendant should be punished by death, but no post-conviction deliberation is required for a life sentence.[45]

The issue surrounding the difference between Section 775.082 (1), Florida Statutes, and the U.S. Supreme Court's decisions in *Graham* and *Miller* was addressed in several appellate cases.[46]

However, the majority opinions in these cases failed to provide definitive direction in regards to available alternatives for the sentencing of juveniles convicted of capitol felonies in Florida.[47] Florida's five district courts of appeal also were split on other *Graham/Miller* – related decisions.

The 2015 Supreme Court of Florida Decisions

On March 19, 2015, the Supreme Court of Florida (SCF) unanimously decided four post-*Graham/Miller* related cases, deciding:

---

[43] Id. at 2474.
[44] Stop Turning Out Prisoners Act, ch. 294, §4(1), 1995 Fla. Laws 2717, 2718; § 775.082 (1), Fla. Stat. (2011).
[45] § 775.082 (1) Fla. Stat. (2011).
[46] Neely v. State, No. 3D10-1716, 2013 WL 1629227 (Fla. 3d DCA, 2013); Hernandez v. State, 117 So.3d 778 (Fla. 3d DCA, 2013); Walling v. State, 105 So.3d 660 (Fla. 1st DCA, 2013); Partlow v. State, No. 1D10-5896, 2013 WL 45743(Fla. 1st DCA, 2013); Washington v. State, 103 So.3d 917, 920 (Fla. 1st DCA, 2012).
[47] Id.

• *Leighdon Henry v. State of Florida*: The Graham decision applies to "term-of-years" prison sentences (not just life imprisonment sentences), because otherwise the sentence of 90 years in this case "will not provide a meaningful opportunity for release" (required by Graham).

The SCF reversed the Fifth DCA's decision, and remanded (sent back) the case to the trial court for resentencing consistent with the court's direction and the new 2014 law passed by the Legislature. (SEE next section). This inmate was 17 years old when he committed his crimes.[48]

• *Rebecca Lee Falcon v. State of Florida*: The *Miller* decision must be given retroactive effect because it constitutes a "development of fundamental significance." The decision is retroactive to "juvenile offenders whose convictions and sentences were final at the time Miller was decided."

The sentence in this case was life without the possibility of parole. The SCF reversed the First DCA's decision, and remanded the case to the trial court for resentencing consistent with the new 2014 law. The inmate was 15 years old when she committed her crimes.[49]

• *Shimeeka Daquiel Gridine v. State of Florida*: The *Graham* decision prohibits sentencing a 14-year-old to a prison sentence of 70 years for the crime of attempted first-murder.

The court ruled such a sentence is unconstitutional because it "does not provide a meaningful opportunity for future release." Reversing the First DCA, the court remanded the case back to the sentencing court.[50]

---

[48] Henry v. Florida, SC12-578 (FLA. March 19, 2015).
[49] Rebecca Lee Falcon v. State of Florida , SC13-865 (FLA. March 19, 2015).
[50] Shimeeka Daquiel Gridine v. State of Florida SC12-1223 (FLA. March 19, 2015).

• *Anthony Duwayne Horsley, Jr. v. State of Florida*: The *Miller* decision means the proper remedy is to apply the 2014 Florida law to "all juvenile offenders whose sentences are unconstitutional under *Miller*."

Citing the "unequivocal expression of legislative intent" by the 2014 law, the court ruled it "provides for individualized sentencing consideration prior to imposition of a life sentence on a juvenile offender," and rejected the state's argument to maintain the original sentence through the "revival" of a 20 year-old sentencing law. The sentence in this case was life without the possibility of parole. This inmate was 17 years old when he committed his crimes.[51]

The 2014 Florida Law

Ch. 14-220, Laws of Florida (HB 7035) addresses the *Graham* and *Miller* decisions by specifying that a juvenile offender convicted of a:

• *Capital felony* homicide offense where the person actually killed, intended to kill, or attempted to kill the victim *must* be sentenced to life if the judge, after considering specified factors at a mandatory sentencing hearing (sentencing hearing), determines that life is appropriate, or *must* be sentenced to a term of at least 40 years if the judge concludes that life is not appropriate.

Such person is entitled to have the court of original jurisdiction (court) review the sentence after 25 years, unless he or she has previously been convicted of an enumerated offense, or conspiracy to commit an enumerated offense;

• *Life felony* homicide offense where the person actually killed, intended to kill, or attempted to kill the victim *may* be sentenced to life if the judge, after considering specified factors at a sentencing hearing, determines that life is appropriate.

---

[51] Anthony Duwayne Horsley, Jr. v. State of Florida SC13-1938 (FLA. March 19, 2015) and State of Florida v. Anthony Duwayne Horsley, Jr. SC13-2000 (FLA. March 19, 2015).

Such person is entitled to have the court review the sentence after 25 years if the juvenile is sentenced to a term of imprisonment of more than 25 years;

• *Capital, life, or first degree felony* homicide offense where the person did not actually kill, intend to kill, or attempt to kill the victim *may* be sentenced to life if the judge, after considering specified factors at a sentencing hearing, determines that life is appropriate.

Such person is entitled to have the court review the sentence after 15 years if the juvenile is sentenced to a term of imprisonment of more than 15 years.

• *Nonhomicide or life felonies or first degree felonies punishable by life* offense *may* be sentenced to life, if the judge, after considering specified factors at a sentencing hearing, determines that life is appropriate.

Such person is entitled to have the court review the sentence after 20 years if the juvenile is sentenced to a term of imprisonment of 20 years or more. The juvenile offender is eligible for one subsequent review hearing 10 years after the initial review hearing.

This chapter discusses legislative and judicial decisions that may impact approximately 1,000 or more current state inmates who have received sentences of 70 years or longer. Arguably sentences of 30 to 70 years also can be challenged.

Civil Citations and Other Diversion Programs

On the front end of the criminal justice system, policymakers have increasingly used civil citations, law enforcement warnings and other diversion programs to keep first-time juvenile non-violent offenders out of criminal court. These successful programs will help thousands of Florida youth each year.

The 2015 Florida Law

Ch. 2015-16, Laws of Florida (CS/SB 378) expands juvenile civil citation by allowing law enforcement to issue up to three civil citations to youth. Previously, a civil citation was only available to youth who admit to committing a first-time misdemeanor.

In addition, law enforcement will be authorized to:

- Issue a simple warning to the youth (law enforcement has always been able to do this);
- Inform the youth's parents of the misdemeanor (law enforcement has always been able to do this);
- Issue a civil citation; or
- Require participation in a similar diversion program under the bill.

The law also states that if an arrest is made, law enforcement must provide written documentation as to why the arrest is warranted.

During the last four years the use of civil citations has expanded from seven to 60 counties (Florida has 67 counties). The key to continued success will be how Florida's law enforcement and state agencies implement the new law, including training officers on civil citation. (DJJ already has a centralized database system)

Public Policy Research

A recent report[52] sponsored by the Children's Campaign and authored by Dewey Caruthers, one of the state's top civil citation experts, found:

---

[52] Dewey & Associates, The Children's Campaign, Joseph W. Terrell S. Clark, Stepping Up: Florida's Top Civil Citation Efforts. Advocating the Importance of Civil Citations While Recognizing Those That Do it Best, Project on Accountable Justice; The James Madison Institute; Southern Poverty Law Center (2015), http://iamforkids.org/wp-content/uploads/2015/07/Stepping-Up-Floridas-Top-Civil- Citation-Efforts-7-09-15.pdf

1. A 25 percent increase in the use of civil citations as alternatives to arrest would save taxpayers as much as $61 million -- while keeping kids from handicapping their futures because of common misbehavior such as fighting, under-drinking or using illegal drugs.

2. Being arrested as a juvenile can impact employment, post-secondary education, housing and loans for the rest of the offenders' lives.

3. The use of civil citations has grown enormously in Florida over the past four years. They offer law enforcement officers the option of diverting teens into mandatory community service for certain offenses that are common youth misbehavior.

Additionally, offenders are required to write letters of apology to the victims and sometimes to law officers. Most importantly, they're also assessed to see whether they are first-time, one-time offenders, or are at-risk to reoffend, And if so, are provided with other services -- such as anger management, family counseling or alcohol and substance-abuse treatment.

4. 21,349 youths were eligible for civil citations in fiscal year 2013-2014, but only 8,059 --- or 38 percent --- received them. Miami-Dade County came in first among Florida counties for its use of civil citations with 91 percent of juvenile cases.

Caruthers credited former Florida Department of Juvenile Justice (DJJ) Secretary Wansley Walters, who pioneered the program in Miami-Dade before Gov. Rick Scott appointed her to head DJJ in 2011.

5. Four years ago, seven Florida counties had civil-citation pro-grams. Today, according to the report, the only counties without them are Polk, Manatee, Sarasota, Suwannee, Hardee, Calhoun, Dixie, Gulf, Washington, Bradford and Taylor.

6. The savings of using civil citations are $1,467 to $4,614 per juvenile. It cites earlier work, including a 2010 report by Associated Industries of Florida, which found that processing

offenders through the juvenile-justice system cost $5,000, while issuing a civil citation cost $386.

7. A 2011 report by the Florida TaxWatch Center for Smart Justice put taxpayer savings from the use of civil citations at $44 million to $139 million annually. Other groups calling to expand the use of civil citations included the Project on Accountable Justice at Florida State University, the Southern Poverty Law Center and the James Madison Institute.

CHAPTER FIFTEEN

CALL TO ACTION! GET STARTED NOW

You now have some information to act on your own or with a lawyer. You should take these next three steps:

1. Complete and submit the brief form below, then either:

   • Email it to reggie@floridaclemencylawyer.com

   • Mail it to P.O. Box 11069, Tallahassee, FL, 32302, or

   • Fax it to 850-222-3957

Once the form is received, you'll be eligible to get updates of this book and future legal articles on these subjects.

2. Submit the information below. Or contact the author to request a telephone conference regarding the information contained in this book.

- -

Your Contact Information

Name: _____

D.C. Number (if applicable): _____

Cell phone: _____

Address: _____

_____

Date of Birth: _____

Email address: _____

Relative's or Supporter's Contact Information:

Name: _____

Home phone: _____

Cell phone: _____

Address: _____

_____

Email address: _____

ABOUT THE AUTHOR

Photo by Katrice Howell

Reggie Garcia, Esq. is an AV Preeminent®-rated attorney by Martindale-Hubbell, having achieved the rating agency's **highest marks** for both competency and ethics. He is also an experienced state government lobbyist.

His first book, *How to Leave Prison Early: Florida Clemency, Parole and Work Release*, was published in January 2015.

Described by the media as an "expert in clemency and parole cases," he has visited 30 state prisons. A frequent public speaker, he has appeared on national network and cable TV news programs, and on Florida broadcast affiliate TV stations. He's been interviewed on the radio, and has had many articles published in legal magazines and newspapers.

Reggie graduated in 1982 from the University of Florida College of Journalism and Communications. In 1985, he graduated from the University of Florida Levin College of Law where he was the president of the leadership honorary society Florida Blue Key, and a member of the UF Hall of Fame. A native of Tampa, Florida, he currently resides in Tallahassee.

Second Chances

Connect with Reggie Garcia:

Email: reggie@floridaclemencylawyer.com

Website: www.FloridaClemencyLawyer.com

Facebook: facebook.com/reggiegarcia

Twitter: @clemencylawyer

Address: P.O. Box 11069, Tallahassee, FL 32302

Fax: (850) 222-3957

APPENDIX A

Executive Clemency Applications Granted at Clemency Board Meetings Between February 1, 2011 and December 10, 2014

BOARD ACTION DATE	Restoration of Civil Rights	Alien Status under FL Law (With Hearing)	COS Regular	Firearm Authority	Full Pardon	Pardon for Misdemeanor	Pardon w/o Firearm Authority	Total
02/24/11	2			1	1			3
06/02/11	10			5	2	1		18
09/21/11	13	1		4	1			19
12/16/11	8			4	5		1	18
03/22/12	11			2	3	2		18
06/28/12	20			5	9			34
09/20/12	12			4	6	1		23
12/13/12	9			4	6	1		20
03/20/13	14			3	4		1	22
06/26/13	18			9	10		1	38
09/25/13	17			11	7	2		37
12/12/13	24		1	7	4			36
03/19/14	18			4	5			27
06/18/14	16			3	9			28
09/23/14	7			8	5			20
12/10/14	16			4	11			*31
Total	215	1	1	78	88	7	3	392

The data in this table represents 348 distinct clemency applicants who were granted 392 types of clemency (i.e., one application may have been granted Restoration of Civil Rights and a Full Pardon at one meeting).

*The 31 distinct applicants in the 12/10/14 meeting were granted, but are awaiting Board signatures.

APPENDIX B

Florida Rules of Executive Clemency
Revised - March 9, 2011

TABLE OF CONTENTS

E. Restoration of Civil Rights or Alien Status under Florida Law

6. APPLICATIONS

A. Application Forms

B. Supporting Documents

C. Applicant Responsibility

D. Failure to Meet Requirements

E. Notification

7. APPLICATIONS REFERRED TO THE FLORIDA COMMISSION ON OFFENDER REVIEW

8. COMMUTATION OF SENTENCE

A. Request for Review

B. Referral to Commission

C. Notification

D. § 944.30 Cases

E. Domestic Violence Case Review

9. RESTORATION OF CIVIL RIGHTS OR ALIEN STATUS UNDER FLORIDA LAW WITHOUT A HEARING

A. Criteria for Eligibility

B. Action by Clemency Board

C. Out-of-State or Federal Convictions

10. RESTORATION OF CIVIL RIGHTS OR ALIEN STATUS UNDER FLORIDA LAW WITH A HEARING

A. Criteria for 7 Year Eligibility

B. Out-of-State or Federal Convictions

11. HEARINGS BY THE CLEMENCY BOARD ON PENDING APPLICATIONS

A. Cases on the Agenda

RULES OF EXECUTIVE CLEMENCY

1. <u>Statement of Policy</u>

Executive Clemency is a power vested in the Governor by the Florida Constitution of 1968. Article IV, Section 8(a) of the Constitution provides:

> Except in cases of treason and in cases where impeachment results in conviction, the governor may, by executive order filed with the custodian of state records, suspend collection of fines and forfeitures, grant reprieves not exceeding sixty days and, with the approval of two members of the cabinet, grant full or conditional pardons, restore civil rights, commute punishment, and remit fines and forfeitures for offenses.

The Governor and members of the Cabinet collectively are the Clemency Board. Clemency is an act of mercy that absolves the individual upon whom it is bestowed from all or any part of the punishment that the law imposes.

2. <u>Administration</u>

A. These rules were created by mutual consent of the Clemency Board to assist persons in applying for clemency. However, nothing contained herein can or is intended to limit the authority or discretion given to the Clemency Board in the exercise of its constitutional prerogative.

B. The Office of Executive Clemency was created to assist in the orderly and expeditious exercise of this executive power.

C. The Governor, with the approval of at least two members of the Clemency Board, appoints a Coordinator who hires all assistants. The Coordinator and assistants comprise the Office of Executive Clemency. The Coordinator must keep a proper record of all proceedings and is the custodian of all records.

3. <u>Parole and Probation</u>

The Clemency Board will neither grant nor revoke parole or probation.

4. Clemency

The Governor has the unfettered discretion to deny clemency at any time, for any reason. The Governor, with the approval of at least two members of the Clemency Board, has the unfettered discretion to grant, at any time, for any reason, the following forms of clemency:

I. Types of Clemency

A. Full Pardon

A Full Pardon unconditionally releases a person from punishment and forgives guilt for any Florida convictions. It restores to an applicant all of the rights of citizenship possessed by the person before his or her conviction, including the right to own, possess, or use firearms.

B. Pardon Without Firearm Authority

A Pardon Without Firearm Authority releases a person from punishment and forgives guilt. It entitles an applicant to all of the rights of citizenship enjoyed by the person before his or her conviction, except the specific authority to own, possess, or use firearms.

C. Pardon for Misdemeanor

A Pardon for a Misdemeanor Conviction releases a person from punishment and forgives guilt.

D. Commutation of Sentence

A Commutation of Sentence may adjust an applicant's penalty to one less severe but does not restore any civil rights, and it does not restore the authority to own, possess, or use firearms. (See also Rule 15 on commutation of death sentences.)

E. Remission of Fines and Forfeitures

A Remission of Fines or Forfeitures suspends, reduces, or removes fines or forfeitures.

F. Specific Authority to Own, Possess, or Use Firearms

The Specific Authority to Own, Possess, or Use Firearms restores to an applicant the right to own, possess, or use firearms, which were lost as a result of a felony conviction. Due to federal firearms laws, the Clemency Board will not consider requests for firearm authority from individuals convicted in federal or out-of-state courts. In order to comply with the federal laws, a Presidential Pardon or a Relief of Disability from the Bureau of Alcohol, Tobacco and Firearms must be issued in cases involving federal court convictions. A pardon or restoration of civil rights with no restrictions on firearms must be issued by the state where the conviction occurred.

G. Restoration of Civil Rights in Florida

The Restoration of Civil Rights restores to an applicant all of the rights of citizenship in the State of Florida enjoyed before the felony conviction, except the specific authority to own, possess, or use firearms. Such restoration shall not relieve an applicant from the registration and notification requirements or any other obligations and restrictions imposed by law upon sexual predators or sexual offenders.

H. Restoration of Alien Status under Florida Law

The Restoration of Alien Status Under Florida Law restores to an applicant who is not a citizen of the United States such rights enjoyed by him or her, under the authority of the State of Florida, which were lost as a result of a conviction of any crime that is a felony or would be a felony under Florida law, except the specific authority to own, possess, or use firearms. However, restoration of these rights shall not affect the immigration status of the applicant (i.e., a certificate evidencing Restoration of Alien Status Under Florida Law shall not be a ground for relief from removal proceedings initiated by the United States Immigration and Naturalization Service).

I. Conditional Clemency

All of the preceding forms of clemency may be granted subject to various conditions. If the conditions of clemency are violated or breached, such clemency may be revoked by the Clemency Board, returning the applicant to his or her status prior to receiving the conditional clemency.

5. Eligibility

A. Pardons

A person may not apply for a pardon unless he or she has completed all sentences imposed for the applicant's most recent felony conviction and all conditions of supervision imposed for the applicant's most recent felony conviction have expired or been completed, including but not limited to, parole, probation, community control, control release and conditional release, for a period of no less than 10 years.

The applicant may not have outstanding detainers, or any pecuniary penalties or liabilities which total more than $1,000 and result from any criminal conviction or traffic infraction. In addition, the applicant may not have any outstanding victim restitution, including, but not limited to, restitution pursuant to a court order or civil judgment, or obligations pursuant to Chapter 960, Florida Statutes.

Persons who had adjudication of guilt withheld and were not convicted may apply for a pardon if they otherwise meet the eligibility requirements of this rule.

B. Commutations of Sentence

A person may not be considered for a commutation of sentence unless he or she has been granted a Request for Review pursuant to Rule 8 or has had his or her case placed upon a Clemency Board agenda pursuant to Rule 17.

C. Remission of Fines and Forfeitures

A person may not apply for a remission of fines and forfeitures unless he or she has completed all sentences imposed and all conditions of supervision have expired or been completed, including, but not limited to, parole, probation, community control, control release, and conditional release.

D. Specific Authority to Own, Possess, or Use Firearms

A person may not apply for the specific authority to own, possess, or use firearms unless he or she has completed all sentences imposed for the applicant's most recent felony conviction and all conditions of supervision imposed for the applicant's most recent felony conviction have expired or been completed, including but not limited to, parole, probation, community control, control release, and conditional release, for a period of no less than eight (8) years.

The applicant may not have outstanding detainers, or any pecuniary penalties or liabilities which total more than $1,000 and result from any criminal conviction or traffic infraction. In addition, the applicant may not have any outstanding victim restitution, including, but not limited to, restitution pursuant to a court order or civil judgment, or obligations pursuant to Chapter 960, Florida Statutes. Persons convicted in a federal, military, or out-of-state court are not eligible to apply.

E. Restoration of Civil Rights or Alien Status under Florida Law

A person who meets the requirements of Rule 9 may have his or her civil rights restored by the Clemency Board. Persons who do not qualify for restoration of civil or alien rights under Rule 9 may request restoration of civil rights pursuant to Rule 6 if the person has completed all sentences imposed and all conditions of supervision have expired or been completed, including but not limited to, imprisonment, parole, probation, community control, control release, and conditional release; has no pending outstanding detainers or pending criminal charges; has paid all restitution pursuant to a court order or civil judgment and obligations pursuant to Chapter 960, Florida Statutes; and has met the seven (7) year time requirement. Restoration of civil rights includes all rights of citizenship enjoyed by the person before his or her conviction, except the specific authority to own, possess or use firearms.

If the person was convicted in a court other than a court of the State of Florida, he or she must be a legal resident of the State of Florida at the time the application is filed, considered, and acted upon. If the person is applying for Restoration of Alien Status under Florida Law, he or she must be domiciled in the State of Florida at the time the application is filed, considered, and acted upon.

Notwithstanding any provision of this rule, an individual who has previously had his or her civil rights or Alien Status under Florida Law restored and is subsequently convicted of any offense listed in Rule 9(A) shall be ineligible for restoration of civil rights or Alien Status under Florida law for a period of no less than seven (7) years after completing all sentences and conditions of supervision (including but not limited to, parole, probation, community control, control release and conditional release) arising from the subsequent conviction.

6. Applications

A. Application Forms

All correspondence regarding an application for clemency should be addressed to Coordinator, Office of Executive Clemency, 4070 Esplanade Way, Tallahassee, Florida, 32399-2450. Those persons seeking clemency shall complete an application and submit it to the Office of Executive Clemency.

Persons seeking Restoration of Civil Rights or Alien Status under Florida Law must submit an application. Application forms will be furnished by the Coordinator upon request or they may be downloaded from the clemency website at www.fcor.state.fl.us. All applications for clemency must be filed with the Coordinator on the form provided by the Office of Executive Clemency.

B. Supporting Documents

Each application for clemency shall have attached to it a certified copy of the charging instrument (indictment, information, or warrant with supporting affidavit) for each felony conviction, or misdemeanor conviction if seeking a pardon for a misdemeanor, and a certified copy of the judgment and sentence for each felony conviction, or misdemeanor conviction if seeking a pardon for a misdemeanor.

(Note: The Office of Executive Clemency or Commission on Offender Review may assist in preparation of applications in unique situations.) Each application for clemency may include character references, letters of support, and any other documents that are relevant to the application for clemency.

C. Applicant Responsibility

It is the responsibility of the applicant to answer all inquiries fully and truthfully and to keep the Office of Executive Clemency advised of any change in the information provided in the application, including change of address and phone number.

D. Failure to Meet Requirements

If any application fails to meet the requirements of the Rules of Executive Clemency, the Coordinator may return it without further consideration.

E. Notification

Upon receipt of a completed application that meets the requirements of the Rules of Executive Clemency, the Coordinator shall make reasonable attempts to notify the victims of record, the respective State Attorney's Office, the Office of the Statewide Prosecutor, if applicable, and the Office of the Attorney General, Bureau of Advocacy and Grants.

7. Applications Referred to the Florida Commission on Offender Review

Every application which meets the requirements of these Rules may be referred to the Florida Commission on Offender Review for an investigation, report, and recommendation.

All persons who submit applications shall comply with the reasonable requests of the Florida Commission on Offender Review in order to facilitate and expedite investigation of their cases. Failure to comply with such requests by the Commission, without adequate explanation, may result in denial of the application without further consideration.

8. Commutation of Sentence

A. Request for Review

An applicant who applies for commutation of sentence under Rule 5(B) may do so only if he or she has completed at least one third of the sentence imposed, or, if serving a minimum mandatory sentence, has completed at least one half of the sentence.

Individuals eligible for commutation of sentence consideration may receive a "Request for Review" form by contacting the Office of Executive Clemency or it may be downloaded from the clemency website at www.fcor.state.fl.us. Upon receipt of the Request for Review form, clemency application, and any other material to be considered, the Coordinator shall forward copies of the documents to the Clemency Board and the Florida Commission on Offender Review. The Commission shall review the documents and make an advisory recommendation to the Clemency Board. Notification of receipt by the Office of Executive Clemency of such a request shall be provided as indicated under Rule 6.

Rule 17 may also be invoked by any member of the Clemency Board.

B. Referral to Commission

Upon receipt by the Coordinator of written notification from the Governor and at least one member of the Clemency Board granting a Request for Review, or notification invoking Rule 17, the Coordinator may refer the request to the Commission on Offender Review for a full investigation and place the case on an agenda to be heard by the Clemency Board.

C. Notification

The Coordinator shall attempt to provide individuals seeking a request for commutation of sentences, and the respective prosecuting authority, with approximately 20 days notice prior to any such request being heard by representatives of the Clemency Board.

D. § 944.30 Cases

All remaining § 944.30, Florida Statutes, cases will be processed under this rule.

E. Domestic Violence Case Review

Domestic violence cases that meet the criteria adopted by the Clemency Board on December 18, 1991, as amended, will be processed as requests for review.

9. Restoration of Civil Rights or Alien Status under Florida Law Without a Hearing

A. Criteria for Eligibility

A person may have his or her civil rights or alien status under Florida Law restored by approval of the Clemency Board, excluding the specific authority to own, possess, or use firearms, without a hearing if the person has committed no crimes and has not been arrested for a misdemeanor or felony for five (5) years from the date of completion of all sentences and conditions of supervision imposed and the following requirements are met:

1. The person has completed all sentences imposed and all conditions of supervision have expired or been completed, including but not limited to, imprisonment, parole, probation, community control, control release, and conditional release;

2. The person has no outstanding detainers or pending criminal charges;

3. The person has paid all restitution pursuant to a court order or civil judgment and obligations pursuant to Chapter 960, Florida Statutes;

4. The person has never been convicted of one of the following crimes:

a. murder, attempted murder, attempted felony murder, manslaughter (F.S. Chapter 782);

b. DUI manslaughter, DUI Serious Bodily Injury (F.S. 316.193);

c. leaving the Scene of Accident involving Injury or Death;

d. sexual battery, attempted sexual battery, unlawful sexual activity with a minor, female genital mutilation (F.S. Chapter 794)

e. any violation of F.S. Chapter 800;

f. lewd or lascivious offense upon or in the presence of an elderly or disabled person, attempted lewd or lascivious offense upon or in the presence of an elderly or disabled person (F.S. 825.1025);

g. sexual performance by a child, attempted sexual performance by a child (F.S. 827.071);

h. aggravated child abuse (F.S. 827.03);

i. failure to register as a sexual predator (F.S. 775) or sexual offender (F.S. 943.0435);

j. computer pornography, transmission of computer pornography, or any crime involving a minor in violation of F.S. Chapter 847;

k. kidnapping, attempted kidnapping, false imprisonment, or luring and enticing a child (F.S. Chapter 787);

l. aggravated battery, attempted aggravated battery (F.S. 784.045), felony battery, domestic battery by strangulation (F.S. 784.041);

m. robbery, carjacking, attempted carjacking, home invasion, attempted home invasion (F.S. Chapter 812);

n. poisoning of food or water (F.S. 859.01);

o. abuse of a dead human body (F.S. 872.06);

p. burglary of a dwelling, first degree burglary, or attempted first degree burglary (F.S. 810.02);

q. arson, attempted arson, or conspiracy to commit arson (F.S. 806.01);

r. aggravated assault (F.S. 784.021);

s. aggravated stalking (F.S. 784.048);

t. aggravated battery, battery, or aggravated assault on a law enforcement officer or other specified officer (F.S. 784.07);

u. trafficking or conspiracy to traffic in illegal substances (F.S. 893.135); all other first and second degree felonies described in F. S. Chapter 893.

v. aircraft piracy (F.S. 860.16);

w. unlawful throwing, placing, or discharging of a destructive device or bomb (F.S. 790.161);

x. facilitating or furthering terrorism (F.S. 775.31);

y. treason (F.S. 876.32);

z. possession of a firearm by a convicted felon (F.S. 790.23) or possession of a firearm or ammunition by a violent career criminal (F.S. 790.235);

aa. bribery, misuse of public office (F.S. Chapter 838); extortion by officers of the state (F. S. 839.11); misappropriations of moneys by commissioners to make sales (F.S. 839.17);

bb. any crime committed by an elected official while in office;

cc. illegal use of explosives;

dd. RICO;

ee. exploitation of the elderly;

ff. public corruption;

gg. any felony violation of an election law;

hh. any crime designated a "dangerous crime" under F.S. 907.041;

ii. any offense committed in another jurisdiction that would be an offense listed in this paragraph if that offense had been committed in this State;

5. The person has not been declared to be one of the following:

a. Habitual Violent Felony Offender under F.S. 775.084(1)(b);

b. Three-time Violent Felony Offender under F.S. 775.084(1)(c);

c. Violent Career Criminal under F.S. 775.084;

d. Prison Releasee Reoffender under F.S. 775.082(9)(a);

e. Sexual Predator under F.S. 775.21;

6. In the case of restoration of civil rights, (a) the person must be a citizen of the United States; and (b) if convicted in a court other than a Florida court, the person must be a legal resident of Florida;

7. In the case of restoring alien status under Florida Law, the person must be domiciled in Florida.

B. Action by Clemency Board

The Florida Commission on Offender Review shall accept and retain the records of individuals released by the Department of Corrections by expiration of sentence or from community supervision. In a manner approved by the Board of Clemency, the Commission on Offender Review may provide individuals released by the Department of Corrections with a written explanation of the Rules determining eligibility to apply for restoration of civil rights.

The Commission on Offender Review shall review the applications of individuals who have applied for restoration of civil rights pursuant to Rule 6. If an individual meets all requirements under Rule 9(A), then the Coordinator shall issue a preliminary review list of individuals eligible for restoration of civil rights or alien status under Florida law without a hearing to the Clemency Board members.

If the Governor plus two members approve an individual's restoration of civil rights or alien status under Florida law without a hearing within 60 days of issuance of the preliminary review list, the Coordinator shall, pursuant to executive order, issue a certificate that grants the individual restoration of civil rights or alien status under Florida law in the State of Florida, without the specific authority to own, possess, or use firearms. Article IV, Section 8 of the Florida Constitution provides that an executive order granting clemency requires the signature of the Governor and two members of the Florida Cabinet. If approval is not granted, that candidate will be notified, and may elect to pursue restoration of civil rights with a hearing pursuant to Rule 10.

C. Out-of-State or Federal Convictions

If the person has been convicted in a court other than a court of the State of Florida, a request for the restoration of civil rights or alien status under Florida law must be submitted in accordance with Rule 6. Such request shall be reviewed by the Florida Commission on Offender Review to determine if the requirements under Rule 9(A) are met. If the Commission certifies that all of the requirements in Rule 9(A) are met, the Coordinator shall follow procedures for the restoration of civil rights as enumerated herein.

10. Restoration of Civil Rights or Alien Status under Florida Law With a Hearing

A. Criteria for Seven (7) Year Eligibility

An individual who does not qualify to be granted clemency under Rule 9 must comply with Rule 6 by filing an application to have his or her civil rights or alien status under Florida law restored, excluding the specific authority to own, possess, or use firearms, with a hearing.

An individual is eligible to apply only if the following requirements are met:

1. The person has had no new felony convictions for a period of seven (7) years or more after completion of all sentences imposed for the applicant's most recent felony conviction and all conditions of supervision for the applicant's most recent felony conviction have expired or been completed, including but not limited to, imprisonment, parole, probation, community control, control release, and conditional release;

2. The person has paid all restitution pursuant to a court order or civil judgment and obligations pursuant to Chapter 960, Florida Statutes;

3. In the case of restoration of civil rights, (a) the person must be a citizen of the United States; and (b) if convicted in a court other than a Florida court, the person must be a legal resident of Florida;

4. In the case of restoring alien status under Florida Law, the person must be domiciled in Florida.

B. Out-of-State or Federal Convictions

If the person has been convicted in a court other than a court of the State of Florida, a request for the restoration of civil rights or alien status under Florida law must be submitted in accordance with Rule 6. Such request shall be reviewed by the Florida Commission on Offender Review to determine if the requirements under Rule 10(A) are met. If the Commission certifies that all of the requirements in Rule 10(A) are met, the Coordinator shall follow procedures for the restoration of civil rights or alien status with a hearing as enumerated herein.

11. Hearings by the Clemency Board on Pending Applications

A. Cases on the Agenda

After the Commission on Offender Review investigation is complete, the Coordinator may place upon the agenda for consideration by the Clemency Board at its next scheduled meeting:

1. Timely applications that meet the eligibility requirements under Rule 5 for which any investigation, report and recommendation, conducted under Rule 7, has been completed;

2. Cases in which an applicant has requested a commutation of sentence under Rule 8 or when Rule 17 has been invoked so long as any investigation, report and recommendation conducted under Rule 7 has been completed.

B. Distribution of Agenda

The Coordinator shall prepare an agenda which shall include all cases that qualify for a hearing under Subsection A of this Rule. A preliminary agenda shall be distributed to the

Clemency Board at least 10 days before the next scheduled meeting.

C. Failure of Applicant to Comply With Rules

An applicant's failure to comply with any rule of executive clemency may result in refusal, without notice, to place an application on the agenda for consideration.

12. Hearings Before the Clemency Board

A. Scheduled Meetings

The Clemency Board will meet in the months of March, June, September, and December of each year, or at such times as set by the Clemency Board. The Governor may call a special meeting at any time for any reason.

B. Notice of Appearance

While applicants are not required to appear at the hearing, the Clemency Board encourages applicants to attend. The applicant, or any other person intending to speak on behalf of the applicant, must notify the Office of Executive Clemency at least 10 days prior to the scheduled meeting of the Clemency Board.

C. Time Limits

Any person making an oral presentation to the Clemency Board will be allowed no more than five minutes. All persons making oral presentations in favor of an application shall be allowed cumulatively no more than 10 minutes. All persons making oral presentations against an application, including victims, shall be allowed cumulatively no more than 10 minutes.

D. Filing of Executive Orders

Subsequent to the hearings of the Clemency Board, the Coordinator shall prepare executive orders granting clemency as directed and circulate them to the members of the Clemency Board. After the Executive Orders are fully executed, the Coordinator shall certify and mail a copy to the applicant. The original executive order shall be filed with the custodian of state records. The Coordinator shall send a letter to each applicant officially stating the disposition of his or her application. A seal is not used by the Office of Executive Clemency.

13. Continuance and Withdrawal of Cases

An interested party may apply for a continuance of a case if the continuance is based on good cause. The Governor will decide if the case will be continued. Cases held under advisement for further information desired by the Governor will be marked "continued" and noted on each subsequent agenda until the case is decided.

The applicant may withdraw his or her application by notifying the Office of Executive Clemency at least 20 days prior to the next scheduled meeting of the Clemency Board. A request to withdraw a case made within 20 days of the hearing on the application will be allowed if the Governor or the Coordinator for the Office of Executive Clemency determines that there is good cause. Cases that are withdrawn from the agenda will not be considered again until the application is re-filed.

14. Reapplication for Clemency

Any otherwise eligible person who has been granted or denied any form of executive clemency may not reapply for further executive clemency for at least two (2) years from the date that such action became final. Any person who has been denied a Rule 8 commutation of sentence may not apply for another request for at least five (5) years from the date the prior request was denied.

15. Commutation of Death Sentences

This Rule applies to all cases where the sentence of death has been imposed. The Rules of Executive Clemency, except Rules 1, 2, 3, 4, 15 and 16 are inapplicable to cases where inmates are sentenced to death.

A. Confidentiality

Notwithstanding incorporation of Rule 16 by reference in cases where inmates are sentenced to death, the full text of Rule 16 is repeated below for clarification: Due to the nature of the information presented to the Clemency Board, all records and documents generated and gathered in the clemency process as set forth in the Rules of Executive Clemency are confidential and shall not be made available for inspection to any person except members of the Clemency Board and their staff.

Only the Governor and no other member of the Clemency Board, nor any other state entity that may be in the possession of Clemency Board materials, has the discretion to allow such records and documents to be inspected or copied. Access to such materials shall not constitute a waiver of confidentiality.

B. Commission on Offender Review Investigation

In all cases where the death penalty has been imposed, the Florida Commission on Offender Review may conduct a thorough and detailed investigation into all factors relevant to the issue of clemency and provide a final report to the Clemency Board. The investigation shall include, but not be limited to, (1) an interview with the inmate, who may have clemency counsel present, by the Commission; (2) an interview, if possible, with the trial attorneys who prosecuted the case and defended the inmate; (3) an interview, if possible, with the presiding judge and; (4) an interview, if possible, with the defendant's family.

The Commission on Offender Review shall provide notice to the Office of the Attorney General, Bureau of Advocacy and Grants, that an investigation has been initiated. The Office of the Attorney General, Bureau of Advocacy and Grants shall then provide notice to the victims of record that an investigation is pending and at that time shall request written comments from the victims of record. Upon receipt of comments from victims of record or their representatives, the Office of the Attorney General, Bureau of Advocacy and Grants shall forward such comments to the

Commission on Offender Review to be included in the final report to the Clemency Board.

C. Monitoring Cases for Investigation

The investigation by the Commission on Offender Review shall begin at such time as designated by the Governor. If the Governor has made no such designation, the investigation shall begin immediately after the defendant's initial petition for writ of habeas corpus, filed in the appropriate federal district court, has been denied by the 11th Circuit Court of Appeals, so long as all post-conviction pleadings, both state and federal, have been filed in a timely manner as determined by the Governor.

An investigation shall commence immediately upon any failure to timely file the initial motion for post-conviction relief in state court, and any appeal therefrom, or the initial petition for writ of habeas corpus in federal court, and any appeal therefrom. The time frames established by this rule are not tolled during the pendency of any petition for rehearing or reconsideration (or any similar such motion for clarification, etc.), request for rehearing en banc in the 11th Circuit Court of Appeals, or petition for writ of certiorari in the U.S. Supreme Court.

Failure to conduct or complete the investigation pursuant to these rules shall not be a ground for relief for the death penalty defendant. The Commission on Offender Review's Capital Punishment Research Specialist shall routinely monitor and track death penalty cases beyond direct appeal for this purpose. Cases investigated under previous administrations may be reinvestigated at the Governor's discretion.

D. Commission on Offender Review Report

After the investigation is concluded, the Commissioners who personally interviewed the inmate shall prepare and issue a final report on their findings and conclusions. The final report shall include (1) any statements made by the defendant, and defendant's counsel, during the course of the investigation; (2) a detailed summary from each Commissioner who interviewed the inmate; and (3) information gathered during the course of the investigation. The final report shall be forwarded to all members of the Clemency Board within 120 days of the commencement of the investigation, unless the time period is extended by the Governor.

E. Request for Hearing by any Clemency Board Member

After the report is received by the Clemency Board, the Coordinator shall place the case on the agenda for the next scheduled meeting or at a specially called meeting of the Clemency Board if, as a result of the investigation, or final report, any member of the Clemency Board requests a hearing within 20 days of transmittal of the final report to the Clemency Board. Once a hearing is set, the Coordinator shall provide notice to the appropriate state attorney, the inmate's clemency counsel, the victim's rights coordinator in the Executive Office of the Governor and the Office of Attorney General, Bureau of Advocacy and Grants. The Office of the Attorney General, Bureau of Advocacy and Grants shall then notify the victims of record of the hearing.

F. Request for Hearing by Governor

Notwithstanding any provision to the contrary in the Rules of Executive Clemency, in any case in which the death sentence has been imposed, the Governor may at any time place the case on the agenda and set a hearing for the next scheduled meeting or at a specially called meeting of the Clemency Board.

G. Transcript of Interview

Upon request, a copy of the actual transcript of any statements or testimony of the inmate relating to a clemency investigation shall be provided to the state attorney, the inmate's clemency counsel, or victim's family. The attorney for the state, the inmate's clemency counsel, the victim's family, the inmate, or any other interested person may file a written statement, brief or memorandum on the case within 90 days of initiation of the investigation under Rule 15, copies of which will be distributed to the members of the Clemency Board. The person filing such written information should provide five (5) copies to the Coordinator of the Office of Executive Clemency.

H. Time Limits

At the clemency hearing for capital punishment cases, the inmate's clemency counsel and the attorneys for the state may make an oral presentation, each not to exceed 15 minutes collectively. Representatives of the victim's family may make oral statements not to exceed an additional five minutes collectively. The Governor may extend these time frames at his or her discretion.

I. Distribution and Filing of Orders

If a commutation of a death sentence is ordered by the Governor with the approval of at least two members of the Clemency Board, the original order shall be filed with the custodian of state records, and a copy of the order shall be sent to the inmate, the attorneys representing the state, the inmate's clemency counsel, a representative of the victim's family, the Secretary of the Department of Corrections, and the chief judge of the circuit where the inmate was sentenced. The Office of the Attorney General, Bureau of Advocacy and Grants shall inform the victim's family within 24 hours of such action by the Clemency Board.

16. Confidentiality of Records and Documents

Due to the nature of the information presented to the Clemency Board, all records and documents generated and gathered in the clemency process as set forth in the Rules of Executive Clemency are confidential and shall not be made available for inspection to any person except members of the Clemency Board and their staff. Only the Governor, and no other member of the Clemency Board, nor any other state entity that may be in the possession of Clemency Board materials, has the discretion to allow such records and documents to be inspected or copied. Access to such materials, as approved by the Governor, does not constitute a waiver of confidentiality.

17. Cases Proposed by the Governor or Members of the Clemency Board

In cases of exceptional merit, any member of the Clemency Board may place a case on an upcoming agenda for consideration.

18. Collection of Statistics and Evaluation of Clemency Action

The Office of Executive Clemency, in conjunction with the Florida Commission on Offender Review and Department of Corrections, shall collect and submit to the Clemency Board an annual written report providing statistics and evaluations regarding the status of those individuals whose rights were restored during the previous two calendar years. The first report shall be filed on July 1, 2011.

19. Effective Dates

History. - Adopted September 10, 1975, Rule 6 (formerly Rule 9) effective November 1, 1975; Rule 7 adopted December 8, 1976; Rule 6 amended December 8, 1976, effective July 1, 1977; revised September 14, 1977; Rule 12 amended October 7, 1981; revised December 12, 1984; amended January 8, 1985; amended July 2, 1985; Rule 12 amended September 18, 1986; Rules amended December 18, 1991, effective January 1, 1992; Rule 10 and Rule 15 amended June 22, 1992; Rules amended December 29, 1994, effective January 1, 1995. Rules amended January 7, 1997, effective January 15, 1997; Rule 4 and Rule 9 revised October 28, 1999, effective January 1, 2000; Rules revised June 14, 2001, effective June 14, 2001; Rules revised March 27, 2003; effective March 27, 2003; Rules revised June 20, 2003; effective June 20, 2003; Rules revised December 9, 2004; effective December 9, 2004; Rules revised April 5, 2007, effective April 5, 2007; Rules revised March 9, 2011, effective March 9, 2011.

APPENDIX C

Restoration of Civil Rights' Recidivism Report for 2013-2014 Presented to the Florida Board of Executive Clemency July 1, 2015

FLORIDA COMMISSION ON OFFENDER REVIEW

TENA M. PATE, Chair	RICK SCOTT, Governor
MELINDA N. COONROD, Vice-Chair	PAM BONDI, Attorney General
RICHARD D. DAVISON, Secretary	JEFF ATWATER, Chief Financial Officer
	ADAM PUTNAM, Commissioner of Agriculture

July 1, 2015

The Honorable Rick Scott, Governor
The Honorable Pam Bondi, Attorney General
The Honorable Jeff Atwater, Chief Financial Officer
The Honorable Adam Putnam, Commissioner of Agriculture

Dear Governor Scott, General Bondi, CFO Atwater, and Commissioner Putnam:

Pursuant to the Rules of Executive Clemency, attached is the fifth annual report required by Rule 18 - "Collection of Statistics and Evaluation of Clemency Action."

This report provides information on the status of individuals, whose rights were restored for the previous two calendar years, including recidivism statistics and evaluative data. The felon population reviewed and subsequent data measured includes those individuals whose civil rights were granted during the reporting period and are identified in the clemency database.

If you have any questions regarding the content of this report, please contact me at your convenience at 850-487-1980.

Respectfully,

Tena M. Pate
Chair

Cc:
John Heekin, Assistant General Counsel, Executive Office of the Governor
Carolyn Snurkowski, Associate Deputy Attorney General, Legal Affairs
Robert Tornillo, Director, Cabinet Affairs, Financial Services
Christie Utt, Senior Attorney, Agriculture and Consumer Services

COMMITTED TO PROTECTING THE PUBLIC

RESTORATION OF CIVIL RIGHTS' RECIDIVISM REPORT FOR 2013 & 2014

Presented to the Florida Board of Executive Clemency

July 1, 2015

FLORIDA COMMISSION ON OFFENDER REVIEW

A Governor and Cabinet Agency Created in 1941

The Board of Executive Clemency

Rick Scott, Governor

Pam Bondi, Attorney General

Jeff Atwater, Chief Financial Officer

Adam Putnam, Commissioner of Agriculture and Consumer Services

Florida Commission on Offender Review

The Commission acts as the investigative and administrative arm
of the Board of Executive Clemency.

Mission Statement

To Ensure Public Safety and Provide Victim Assistance
Through the Post Prison Release Process

Commissioners

Tena M. Pate, Chair

Melinda N. Coonrod, Vice Chair

Richard D. Davison, Secretary

Office of Executive Clemency

Julia McCall, Coordinator

Office of Clemency Investigations

Stephen Hebert, Director

Report Overview

Introduction

Pursuant to Rule 18, Rules of Executive Clemency, the Office of Executive Clemency, the Florida Commission on Offender Review, and the Department of Corrections are directed to provide annually, beginning July 1, 2011 and each year thereafter, a report on the status of individuals whose rights were restored for the previous two calendar years, including recidivism statistics and evaluative data.

Rule 18 states:

"18. Collection of Statistics and Evaluation of Clemency Action

The Office of Executive Clemency, in conjunction with the Florida Commission on Offender Review and Department of Corrections, shall collect and submit to the Clemency Board an annual written report providing statistics and evaluations regarding the status of those individuals whose rights were restored during the previous two calendar years. The first report shall be filed on July 1, 2011."[1]

This report provides data on the number of individuals whose civil rights were restored during calendar years 2013 and 2014, along with data indicating the number and percentage of these individuals that have reoffended by committing a new felony conviction subsequent to the date their civil rights were granted by the Clemency Board.

Methodology

TABLE I
All individuals whose civil rights were granted during the reporting period were identified in the Florida Commission on Offender Review's Management of Application for Clemency (MAC) database and are included in this report.

TABLE II
The definition of "reoffend" for this table is any individual who has been convicted of a new felony offense and has returned to the custody of the Florida Department of Corrections (DC), the Federal Bureau of Prisons, a Florida county jail, or another out-of-state entity, subsequent to the date their civil rights were granted by the Clemency Board.

All individuals whose civil rights were granted during the reporting period were reviewed by Commission staff to determine if any new felony convictions occurred subsequent to the date an individual's civil rights were granted. Criminal histories for each individual were reviewed by running queries in three criminal justice databases between June 1-5, 2015. The databases utilized were the Florida Crime Information Center/National Crime Information Center (FCIC/NCIC), the Corrections Data Center (CDC), and the Comprehensive Case Information System (CCIS).

TABLE III
The definition of "reoffend" for this table is any individual who has returned to the custody of the Florida Department of Corrections (DC) subsequent to the date their civil rights were granted by the Clemency Board.

All individuals whose civil rights were granted during the reporting period and are identified by a DC Number in the MAC database were cross-referenced against the DC database on June 16, 2015. Some individuals in the MAC database do not have a DC Number if they only had an out-of-state or federal felony conviction, or a felony conviction which resulted in service of a county jail sentence.

---

1 Florida Rules of Executive Clemency, Rule 18, revised March 9, 2011, effective March 9, 2011.

Data Tables

TABLE I
PERSONS GRANTED RCR
Calendar Years 2013 & 2014

CLEMENCY TYPE	PERSONS GRANTED RCR IN 2013	PERSONS GRANTED RCR IN 2014	TOTAL
Restoration of Civil Rights	569	562	1,131

TABLE II
PERSONS REOFFENDING WITH NEW FELONY CONVICTION
Calendar Years 2013 & 2014

CALENDAR YEAR GRANTED	TOTAL PERSONS GRANTED RCR	TOTAL PERSONS REOFFENDING WITH NEW FELONY CONVICTION	PERCENTAGE OF PERSONS REOFFENDING WITH NEW FELONY CONVICTION
2013	569	4	0.7%
2014	562	1	0.2%
Total	1,131	5	0.4%

TABLE III
PERSONS RETURNED TO FL DC CUSTODY BY REPORT YEAR & CURRENT YEAR

RCR RECIDIVISM REPORT YEAR	CALENDAR YEARS	PERSONS GRANTED RCR	PERSONS RETURNED TO FL DC CUSTODY AT TIME OF ORIGINAL REPORT	PERCENTAGE AT TIME OF ORIGINAL REPORT	PERSONS RETURNED TO DC CUSTODY AS OF 6/16/15	PERCENTAGE AS OF 6/16/15
Jul 01, 2011	2009-2010	30,672	3,406	11.1%	7,829	25.5%
Jul 01, 2012	2010-2011	5,771	651	11.3%	1,365	23.7%
Jul 01, 2013	2011-2012	420	0	0.0%	1	0.2%
Jul 01, 2014	2012-2013	911	1	0.1%	3	0.3%
Jul 01, 2015	2013-2014	1,131	3	0.3%	3	0.3%

Data Tables

PERSONS GRANTED CIVIL RIGHTS THAT WERE RETURNED TO FL DC CUSTODY*

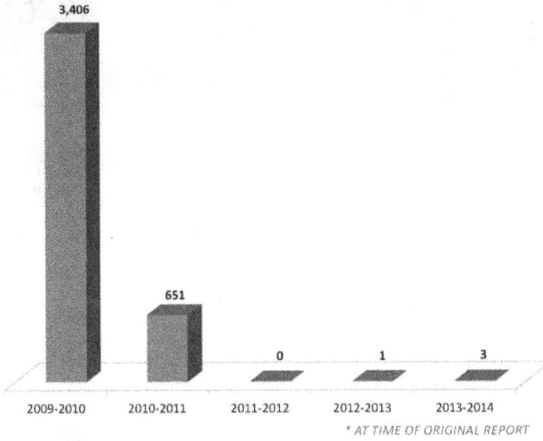

2009-2010	2010-2011	2011-2012	2012-2013	2013-2014
3,406	651	0	1	3

* AT TIME OF ORIGINAL REPORT

PERCENTAGE OF PERSONS GRANTED CIVIL RIGHTS THAT WERE RETURNED TO FL DC CUSTODY*

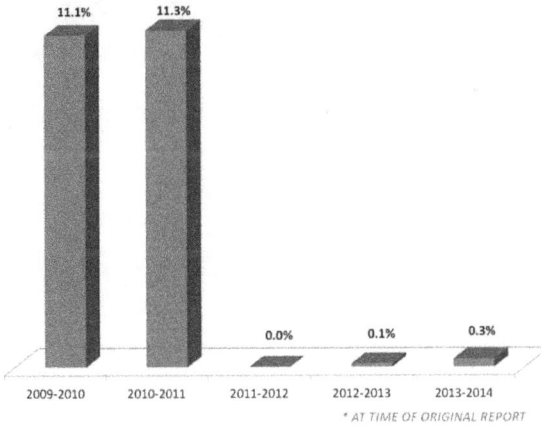

2009-2010	2010-2011	2011-2012	2012-2013	2013-2014
11.1%	11.3%	0.0%	0.1%	0.3%

* AT TIME OF ORIGINAL REPORT

Contact Information

Florida Commission on Offender Review
4070 Esplanade Way
Tallahassee, FL 32399-2450
(850) 922-0000
www.fcor.state.fl.us

For information concerning the contents of this report contact:

Office of Executive Clemency
Julia McCall, Coordinator   (850) 488-2952

Office of Clemency Investigations
Stephen Hebert, Director   (850) 487-1175

For information regarding applications for restoration of civil rights; restoration of alien status under Florida law; pardons; commutation of sentence; remission of fines/forfeitures; and specific authority to own, possess or use firearms, call toll-free (800) 435-8286 or (850) 488-2952 or visit www.fcor.state.fl.us.

Media Inquiries
Press inquiries and public records requests regarding the Florida Commission on Offender Review should be directed to the Communications office at (850) 921-2816 or email publicaffairs@fcor.state.fl.us.

Legislative Inquiries
Legislative inquiries and questions should be directed to the Legislative Affairs office at (850) 921-2816 or email PeterMurray@fcor.state.fl.us.

APPENDIX D

Florida 2011 "De-Coupling" Law

NOTE: CODING: Words stricken are deletions; words underlined are additions.

CHAPTER 2011-207

Committee Substitute for Senate Bill No. 146

An act relating to criminal justice; providing a short title; providing legislative intent; requiring state agencies to prepare reports that identify and evaluate restrictions on licensing and employment for ex-offenders; amending s. 112.011, F.S.; prohibiting state agencies from denying an application for a license, permit, certificate, or employment based solely on a person's lack of civil rights; providing an exception; providing effective dates.

Be It Enacted by the Legislature of the State of Florida:

Section 1. This act may be cited as the "Jim King Keep Florida Working Act."

Section 2. Restrictions on the employment of ex-offenders; legislative intent; state agency reporting requirements.—

(1) The Legislature declares that a goal of this state is to clearly identify the occupations from which ex-offenders are disqualified based on the nature of their offenses. The Legislature seeks to make employment opportunities available to ex-offenders in a manner that serves to preserve and protect the health, safety, and welfare of the general public, yet encourages them to become productive members of society. To this end, state agencies that exercise regulatory authority are in the best position to identify all restrictions on employment imposed by the agencies or by boards

that regulate professions and occupations and are obligated to protect the health, safety, and welfare of the general public by clearly setting forth those restrictions in keeping with standards and protections determined by the agencies to be in the least restrictive manner.

(2) Each state agency, including, but not limited to, those state agencies responsible for professional and occupational regulatory boards, shall ensure the appropriate restrictions necessary to protect the overall health, safety, and welfare of the general public are in place, and by December 31, 2011, and every 4 years thereafter, submit to the Governor, the President of the Senate, and the Speaker of the House of Representatives a report that includes:

(a) A list of all agency or board statutes or rules that disqualify from employment or licensure persons who have been convicted of a crime and have completed any incarceration and restitution to which they have been sentenced for such crime.

(b) A determination of whether the disqualifying statutes or rules are readily available to prospective employers and licensees.

(c) The identification and evaluation of alternatives to the disqualifying statutes or rules which protect the health, safety, and welfare of the general public without impeding the gainful employment of ex-offenders.

Section 3. Effective January 1, 2012, section 112.011, Florida Statutes, is amended to read:

112.011 Disqualification from licensing and public employment based on criminal conviction Felons; removal of disqualifications for employment, exceptions.—

(1)(a) Except as provided in s. 775.16, a person may shall not be disqualified from employment by the state, any of its agencies or political subdivisions, or any municipality solely because of a prior conviction for a crime. However, a person may be denied employment by the state, any of its agencies or political subdivisions, or any municipality by reason of the prior conviction for a crime if the crime was a felony or first degree misdemeanor and directly related to the position of employment sought.

(b) Except as provided in s. 775.16, a person whose civil rights have been restored shall not be disqualified to practice, pursue, or engage in any occupation, trade, vocation, profession, or business for which a license, permit, or certificate is required to be issued by the state, any of its agencies or political subdivisions, or any municipality solely because of a prior conviction for a crime. However, a person whose civil rights have been restored may be denied a license, permit, or certification to pursue, practice, or engage in an occupation, trade, vocation, profession, or business by reason of the prior conviction for a crime if the crime was a felony or first-degree first degree misdemeanor that is and directly related to the standards determined by the regulatory authority to be necessary and reasonably related to the protection of the public health, safety, and welfare for the specific occupation, trade, vocation, profession, or business for which the license, permit, or certificate is sought.

(c) Notwithstanding any law to the contrary, a state agency may not deny an application for a license, permit, certificate, or employment based solely on the applicant's lack of civil rights. However, this paragraph does not apply to applications for a license to carry a concealed weapon or firearm under chapter 790.

(2)(a) This section does shall not apply be applicable to any law enforcement or correctional agency.

(b) This section does shall not apply be applicable to the employment practices of any fire department relating to the hiring of firefighters. An applicant for employment with any fire department who has with a prior felony conviction shall be excluded from employment for a period of 4 years after expiration of sentence or final release by the Parole Commission unless the applicant, before prior to the expiration of the 4-year period, has received a full pardon or has had his or her civil rights restored.

(c) This section does shall not apply be applicable to the employment practices of any county or municipality relating to the hiring of personnel for positions deemed to be critical to security or public safety pursuant to ss. 125.5801 and 166.0442.

(3) Any complaint concerning the violation of this section shall be adjudicated in accordance with the procedures set forth in chapter 120 for administrative and judicial review.

Section 4. Except as otherwise expressly provided in this act, this act shall take effect upon becoming a law.

Approved by the Governor June 21, 2011.

Filed in Office Secretary of State June 21, 2011.

APPENDIX E

Section 960.001, Florida Statutes
Guidelines for Fair Treatment of Victims and Witnesses in the
Criminal Justice and Juvenile Justice Systems

(1) The Department of Legal Affairs, the state attorneys, the Department of Corrections, the Department of Juvenile Justice, the Florida Commission on Offender Review, the State Courts Administrator and circuit court administrators, the Department of Law Enforcement, and every sheriff's department, police department, or other law enforcement agency as defined in s. 943.10(4) shall develop and implement guidelines for the use of their respective agencies, which guidelines are consistent with the purposes of this act and s. 16(b), Art. I of the State Constitution and are designed to implement s. 16(b), Art. I of the State Constitution and to achieve the following objectives:

(a) *Information concerning services available to victims of adult and juvenile crime.*—As provided in s. 27.0065, state attorneys and public defenders shall gather information regarding the following services in the geographic boundaries of their respective circuits and shall provide such information to each law enforcement agency with jurisdiction within such geographic boundaries. Law enforcement personnel shall ensure, through distribution of a victim's rights information card or brochure at the crime scene, during the criminal investigation, and in any other appropriate manner, that victims are given, as a matter of course at the earliest possible time, information about:

1. The availability of crime victim compensation, if applicable;

2. Crisis intervention services, supportive or bereavement counseling, social service support referrals, and community-based victim treatment programs;

3. The role of the victim in the criminal or juvenile justice process, including what the victim may expect from the system as well as what the system expects from the victim;

4. The stages in the criminal or juvenile justice process which are of significance to the victim and the manner in which information about such stages can be obtained;

5. The right of a victim, who is not incarcerated, including the victim's parent or guardian if the victim is a minor, the lawful representative of the victim or of the victim's parent or guardian if the victim is a minor, and the next of kin of a homicide victim, to be informed, to be present, and to be heard when relevant, at all crucial stages of a criminal or juvenile proceeding, to the extent that this right does not interfere with constitutional rights of the accused, as provided by s. 16(b), Art. I of the State Constitution;

6. In the case of incarcerated victims, the right to be informed and to submit written statements at all crucial stages of the criminal proceedings, parole proceedings, or juvenile proceedings; and

7. The right of a victim to a prompt and timely disposition of the case in order to minimize the period during which the victim must endure the responsibilities and stress involved to the extent that this right does not interfere with the constitutional rights of the accused.(b) *Information for purposes of notifying victim or appropriate next of kin of victim or other designated contact of victim.* —In the case of a homicide, pursuant to chapter 782; or a sexual offense, pursuant to chapter 794; or an attempted murder or sexual offense, pursuant to chapter 777; or stalking, pursuant to s. 784.048; or domestic violence, pursuant to s. 25.385:

1. The arresting law enforcement officer or personnel of an organization that provides assistance to a victim or to the appropriate next of kin of the victim or other designated

contact must request that the victim or appropriate next of kin of the victim or other designated contact complete a victim notification card. However, the victim or appropriate next of kin of the victim or other designated contact may choose not to complete the victim notification card.

2. Unless the victim or the appropriate next of kin of the victim or other designated contact waives the option to complete the victim notification card, a copy of the victim notification card must be filed with the incident report or warrant in the sheriff's office of the jurisdiction in which the incident report or warrant originated. The notification card shall, at a minimum, consist of:

a. The name, address, and phone number of the victim; or

b. The name, address, and phone number of the appropriate next of kin of the victim; or

c. The name, address, and telephone number of a designated contact other than the victim or appropriate next of kin of the victim; and

d. Any relevant identification or case numbers assigned to the case.

3. The chief administrator, or a person designated by the chief administrator, of a county jail, municipal jail, juvenile detention facility, or residential commitment facility shall make a reasonable attempt to notify the alleged victim or appropriate next of kin of the alleged victim or other designated contact within 4 hours following the release of the defendant on bail or, in the case of a juvenile offender, upon the release from residential detention or commitment. If the chief administrator, or designee, is unable to contact the alleged victim or appropriate next of kin of the alleged victim or other designated contact by telephone, the chief administrator, or designee, must send to the alleged victim or appropriate next

of kin of the alleged victim or other designated contact a written notification of the defendant's release.

4. Unless otherwise requested by the victim or the appropriate next of kin of the victim or other designated contact, the information contained on the victim notification card must be sent by the chief administrator, or designee, of the appropriate facility to the subsequent correctional or residential commitment facility following the sentencing and incarceration of the defendant, and unless otherwise requested by the victim or the appropriate next of kin of the victim or other designated contact, he or she must be notified of the release of the defendant from incarceration as provided by law.

5. If the defendant was arrested pursuant to a warrant issued or taken into custody pursuant to s. 985.101 in a jurisdiction other than the jurisdiction in which the defendant is being released, and the alleged victim or appropriate next of kin of the alleged victim or other designated contact does not waive the option for notification of release, the chief correctional officer or chief administrator of the facility releasing the defendant shall make a reasonable attempt to immediately notify the chief correctional officer of the jurisdiction in which the warrant was issued or the juvenile was taken into custody pursuant to s. 985.101, and the chief correctional officer of that jurisdiction shall make a reasonable attempt to notify the alleged victim or appropriate next of kin of the alleged victim or other designated contact, as provided in this paragraph, that the defendant has been or will be released.

(c) *Information concerning protection available to victim or witness.*—A victim or witness shall be furnished, as a matter of course, with information on steps that are available to law enforcement officers and state attorneys to protect victims and witnesses from intimidation. Victims of domestic violence shall also be given information about the address confidentiality program provided under s. 741.403.

(d) *Notification of scheduling changes.*—Each victim or witness who has been scheduled to attend a criminal or juvenile justice proceeding shall be notified as soon as possible by the agency scheduling his or her appearance of any change in scheduling which will affect his or her appearance.

(e) *Advance notification to victim or relative of victim concerning judicial proceedings; right to be present.*—Any victim, parent, guardian, or lawful representative of a minor who is a victim, or relative of a homicide victim shall receive from the appropriate agency, at the address found in the police report or the victim notification card if such has been provided to the agency, prompt advance notification, unless the agency itself does not have advance notification, of judicial and post-judicial proceedings relating to his or her case, including all proceedings or hearings relating to:

1. The arrest of an accused;

2. The release of the accused pending judicial proceedings or any modification of release conditions; and

3. Proceedings in the prosecution or petition for delinquency of the accused, including the filing of the accusatory instrument, the arraignment, disposition of the accusatory instrument, trial or adjudicatory hearing, sentencing or disposition hearing, appellate review, subsequent modification of sentence, collateral attack of a judgment, and, when a term of imprisonment, detention, or residential commitment is imposed, the release of the defendant or juvenile offender from such imprisonment, detention, or residential commitment by expiration of sentence or parole and any meeting held to consider such release.

A victim, a victim's parent or guardian if the victim is a minor, a lawful representative of the victim or of the victim's parent or guardian if the victim is a minor, or a victim's next of kin may not be excluded from any portion of any hearing, trial, or proceeding pertaining to the offense based solely on the fact that such person is subpoenaed to testify, unless, upon motion, the court determines such person's presence to be prejudicial. The appropriate agency with respect to notification under subparagraph 1. is the arresting law enforcement agency, and the appropriate agency with respect to notification under subparagraphs 2. and 3. is the Attorney General or state attorney, unless the notification relates to a hearing concerning parole, in which case the appropriate agency is the Florida Commission on Offender Review. The Department of Corrections, the Department of Juvenile Justice, or the sheriff is the appropriate agency with respect to release by expiration of sentence or any other release program provided by law. A victim may waive notification at any time, and such waiver shall be noted in the agency's files.

(f) *Information concerning release from incarceration from a county jail, municipal jail, juvenile detention facility, or residential commitment facility.*—The chief administrator, or a person designated by the chief administrator, of a county jail, municipal jail, juvenile detention facility, or residential commitment facility shall, upon the request of the victim or the appropriate next of kin of a victim or other designated contact of the victim of any of the crimes specified in paragraph (b), make a reasonable attempt to notify the victim or appropriate next of kin of the victim or other designated contact before the defendant's or offender's release from incarceration, detention, or residential commitment if the victim notification card has been provided pursuant to paragraph (b).

If prior notification is not successful, a reasonable attempt must be made to notify the victim or appropriate next of kin of the victim or other designated contact within 4 hours following the release of the defendant or offender from incarceration, detention, or residential commitment. If the defendant is released following sentencing, disposition, or furlough, the chief administrator or designee shall make a reasonable attempt to notify the victim or the appropriate next of kin of the victim or other designated contact within 4 hours following the release of the defendant. If the chief administrator or designee is unable to contact the victim or appropriate next of kin of the victim or other designated contact by telephone, the chief administrator or designee must send to the victim or appropriate next of kin of the victim or other designated contact a written notification of the defendant's or offender's release.

(g) *Consultation with victim or guardian or family of victim.—*

1. In addition to being notified of s. 921.143, the victim of a felony involving physical or emotional injury or trauma or, in a case in which the victim is a minor child or in a homicide, the guardian or family of the victim shall be consulted by the state attorney in order to obtain the views of the victim or family about the disposition of any criminal or juvenile case brought as a result of such crime, including the views of the victim or family about:

a. The release of the accused pending judicial proceedings;

b. Plea agreements;

c. Participation in pretrial diversion programs; and

d. Sentencing of the accused.

2. Upon request, the state attorney shall permit the victim, the victim's parent or guardian if the victim is a minor, the lawful representative of the victim or of the victim's parent or guardian if the victim is a minor, or the victim's next of kin in the case of a homicide to review a copy of the presentence investigation report before the sentencing hearing if one was completed. Any confidential information that pertains to medical history, mental health, or substance abuse and any information that pertains to any other victim shall be redacted from the copy of the report. Any person who reviews the report

pursuant to this paragraph must maintain the confidentiality of the report and may not disclose its contents to any person except statements made to the state attorney or the court.

3. If an inmate has been approved for community work release, the Department of Corrections shall, upon request and as provided in s. 944.605, notify the victim, the victim's parent or guardian if the victim is a minor, the lawful representative of the victim or of the victim's parent or guardian if the victim is a minor, or the victim's next of kin if the victim is a homicide victim.

(h) *Return of property to victim.*—Law enforcement agencies and the state attorney shall promptly return a victim's property held for evidentiary purposes unless there is a compelling law enforcement reason for retaining it. The trial or juvenile court exercising jurisdiction over the criminal or juvenile proceeding may enter appropriate orders to implement this subsection, including allowing photographs of the victim's property to be used as evidence at the criminal trial or the juvenile proceeding in place of the victim's property if no substantial evidentiary issue related thereto is in dispute.

(i) *Notification to employer and explanation to creditors of victim or witness.*— A victim or witness who so requests shall be assisted by law enforcement agencies and the state attorney in informing his or her employer that the need for victim and witness cooperation in the prosecution of the case may necessitate the absence of that victim or witness from work. A victim or witness who, as a direct result of a crime or of his or her cooperation with law enforcement agencies or a state attorney, is subjected to serious financial strain shall be assisted by such agencies and state attorney in explaining to the creditors of such victim or witness the reason for such serious financial strain.

(j) *Notification of right to request restitution.*—Law enforcement agencies and the state attorney shall inform the victim of the victim's right to request and receive restitution pursuant to s. 775.089 or s. 985.437, and of the victim's rights of enforcement under ss. 775.089(6) and 985.0301 in the event an offender does not comply with a restitution order.

The state attorney shall seek the assistance of the victim in the documentation of the victim's losses for the purpose of requesting and receiving restitution. In addition, the state attorney shall inform the victim if and when restitution is ordered. If an order of restitution is converted to a civil lien or civil judgment against the defendant, the clerks shall make available at their office, as well as on their website, information provided by the Secretary of State, the court, or The Florida Bar on enforcing the civil lien or judgment.

(k) *Notification of right to submit impact statement.*—The state attorney shall inform the victim of the victim's right to submit an oral or written impact statement pursuant to s. 921.143 and shall assist in the preparation of such statement if necessary.(l) *Local witness coordination services.*—The requirements for notification provided for in paragraphs (c), (d), and (i) may be performed by the state attorney or public defender for their own witnesses.

(m) *Victim assistance education and training.*—Victim assistance education and training shall be offered to persons taking courses at law enforcement training facilities and to state attorneys and assistant state attorneys so that victims may be promptly, properly, and completely assisted.

(n) *General victim assistance.*—Victims and witnesses shall be provided with such other assistance, such as transportation, parking, separate pretrial waiting areas, and translator services in attending court, as is practicable.

(o) *Victim's rights information card or brochure.*—A victim of a crime shall be provided with a victim's rights information card or brochure containing essential information concerning the rights of a victim and services available to a victim as required by state law.

(p) *Information concerning escape from a state correctional institution, county jail, juvenile detention facility, or residential commitment facility.*—In any case where an offender escapes from a state correctional institution, private correctional facility, county jail, juvenile detention facility, or residential commitment facility, the institution of confinement shall immediately notify the state attorney of the jurisdiction where the criminal charge or petition for delinquency arose and the judge who imposed the sentence of incarceration.

The state attorney shall thereupon make every effort to notify the victim, material witness, parents or legal guardian of a minor who is a victim or witness, or immediate relatives of a homicide victim of the escapee. The state attorney shall also notify the sheriff of the county where the criminal charge or petition for delinquency arose. The sheriff shall offer assistance upon request. When an escaped offender is subsequently captured or is captured and returned to the institution of confinement, the institution of confinement shall again immediately notify the appropriate state attorney and sentencing judge pursuant to this section.

(q) *Presence of victim advocate during discovery deposition; testimony of victim of a sexual offense.*—At the request of the victim or the victim's parent, guardian, or lawful representative, the victim advocate designated by the state attorney's office, sheriff's office, or municipal police department, or one representative from a not-for-profit victim services organization, including, but not limited to, rape crisis centers, domestic violence advocacy groups, and alcohol abuse or substance abuse groups shall be permitted to attend and be present during any deposition of the victim. The victim of a sexual offense shall be informed of the right to have the courtroom cleared of certain persons as provided in s. 918.16 when the victim is testifying concerning that offense

(r) *Implementing crime prevention in order to protect the safety of persons and property, as prescribed in the State Comprehensive Plan.*—By preventing crimes that create victims or further harm former victims, crime prevention efforts are an essential part of providing effective service for victims and witnesses. Therefore, the agencies identified in this subsection may participate in and expend funds for crime prevention, public awareness, public participation, and educational activities directly relating to, and in furtherance of, existing public safety statutes. Furthermore, funds may not be expended for the purpose of influencing public opinion on public policy issues that have not been resolved by the Legislature or the electorate.

(s) *Attendance of victim at same school as defendant.*—If the victim of an offense committed by a juvenile is a minor, the Department of Juvenile Justice shall request information to determine if the victim, or any sibling of the victim, attends or is eligible to attend the same school as the offender. However, if the offender is subject to a presentence investigation by the Department of Corrections, the Department of Corrections shall make such request. If the victim or any sibling of the victim attends or is eligible to attend the same school as that of the offender, the appropriate agency shall notify the victim's parent or legal guardian of the right to attend the sentencing or disposition of the offender and request that the offender be required to attend a different school.

(t) *Use of a polygraph examination or other truth-telling device with victim.*—A law enforcement officer, prosecuting attorney, or other government official may not ask or require an adult, youth, or child victim of an alleged sexual battery as defined in chapter 794 or other sexual offense to submit to a polygraph examination or other truth-telling device as a condition of proceeding with the investigation of such an offense. The refusal of a victim to submit to such an examination does not prevent the investigation, charging, or prosecution of the offense.

(u) *Presence of victim advocates during forensic medical examination.*—At the request of the victim or the victim's parent, guardian, or lawful representative, a victim advocate from a certified rape crisis center shall be permitted to attend any forensic medical examination.

(2) The secretary of the Department of Juvenile Justice, and sheriff, chief administrator, or any of their respective designees, who acts in good faith in making a reasonable attempt to comply with the provisions of this section with respect to timely victim notification, shall be immune from civil or criminal liability for an inability to timely notify the victim or appropriate next of kin of the victim or other designated contact of such information. A good faith effort shall be evidenced by a log entry noting that an attempt was made to notify the victim within the time period specified by this section.

(3) (a) A copy of the guidelines and an implementation plan adopted by each agency shall be filed with the Governor, and subsequent changes or amendments thereto shall be likewise filed when adopted.

(b) A copy of a budget request prepared pursuant to chapter 216 shall also be filed for the sole purpose of carrying out the activities and services outlined in the guidelines

(c) The Governor shall advise state agencies of any statutory changes which require an amendment to their guidelines.

(d) The Executive Office of the Governor shall review the guidelines submitted pursuant to this section:

1. To determine whether all affected agencies have developed guidelines which address all appropriate aspects of this section;

2. To encourage consistency in the guidelines and plans in their implementation in each judicial circuit and throughout the state; and

3. To determine when an agency needs to amend or modify its existing guidelines.

(e) The Executive Office of the Governor shall issue an annual report detailing each agency's compliance or noncompliance with its duties as provided under this section. In addition, the Governor may apply to the circuit court of the county where the headquarters of such agency is located for injunctive relief against any agency which has failed to comply with any of the requirements of this section, which has failed to file the guidelines, or which has filed guidelines in violation of this section, to compel compliance with this section.

(4) The state attorney and one or more of the law enforcement agencies within each judicial circuit may develop and file joint agency guidelines, as required by this section, which allocate the statutory duties among the participating agencies. Responsibility for successful execution of the entire guidelines lies with all parties.

(5) Nothing in this section or in the guidelines adopted pursuant to this section shall be construed as creating a cause of action against the state or any of its agencies or political subdivisions.

(6) Victims and witnesses who are not incarcerated shall not be required to attend discovery depositions in any correctional facility.

(7) The victim of a crime, the victim's parent or guardian if the victim is a minor, and the state attorney, with the consent of the victim or the victim's parent or guardian if the victim is a minor, have standing to assert the rights of a crime victim which are provided by law or s. 16(b), Art. I of the State Constitution.

(8) For the purposes of this section, a law enforcement agency or the office of the state attorney may release any information

deemed relevant to adequately inform the victim if the offense was committed by a juvenile. Information gained by the victim pursuant to this chapter, including the next of kin of a homicide victim, regarding any case handled in juvenile court, must not be revealed to any outside party, except as is reasonably necessary in pursuit of legal remedies.

(9) As used in this section, the term "chief administrator" includes the appropriate chief correctional officers of a county jail or municipal jail, and the appropriate chief administrator of a juvenile detention facility or residential commitment facility.

History.—s. 11, ch. 84-363; s. 79, ch. 85-62; s. 13, ch. 88-96; s. 64, ch. 88-122; s. 1, ch. 88-381; s. 8, ch. 90-211; s. 2, ch. 92-66; s. 15, ch. 92-287; s. 12, ch. 93-37; s. 1, ch. 93-230; s. 20, ch. 94-342; s. 2, ch. 95-160; s. 1, ch. 95-254; s. 1, ch. 96-315; s. 1883, ch. 97-102; s. 1, ch. 98-109; s. 63, ch. 98-280; s. 2, ch. 99-263; s. 7, ch. 99-284; s. 1, ch. 99-373; s. 10, ch. 2001-125; s. 3, ch. 2001-209; s. 2, ch. 2002-56; s. 5, ch. 2003-23; s. 137, ch. 2003-402; s. 89, ch. 2004-265; s. 122, ch. 2006-120; s. 1, ch. 2007-129; s. 56, ch. 2014-191.

DEFINITIONS

Advocate: (*verb*) - To speak or write in favor of; support or urge by argument; recommend publicly; (*noun*) – A person who pleads for or in behalf of another; intercessor.

Affidavit: A written declaration made under oath made before an authorized official.

Aggravating Factor: Any fact or circumstance that increases the severity or culpability of a criminal act.

Appeal: Applying to a higher court for a reversal of the decision of a lower court. There are five courts of appeal in Florida, plus the Supreme Court of Florida.

Board of Executive Clemency (BOEC): The governor, attorney general, chief financial officer and commission of agriculture. All are elected statewide, and limited to two consecutive four-year terms.

Capital Felony: A crime punishable by death, or life imprisonment without parole.

Charging Instrument: Usually a document called a "criminal information" filed by a prosecutor which explains the formal charges; can also be a grand jury indictment.

Clemency: An act of mercy that absolves an individual from all or any part of the punishment that the law imposes.

Concurrent Sentence: When a criminal defendant is convicted of two or more crimes, a judge sentences the defendant to a certain period of time for each crime. Sentences that may all be served at the same time, with the longest period controlling, are concurrent sentences.

Condition Precedent: In a contract, an event which must take place before a party to a contract must perform or do their part.

Conditional Medical Release: Conditional Medical Release means the release of an inmate from incarceration by the FCOR when they have been referred by the Department of Corrections, because of an existing medical or physical condition, to be either permanently incapacitated or terminally ill.

Conditional Release: All offenders whose crimes were committed on or after October 1, 1988, which crime fell under the violent offense categories of the Florida Rules of Criminal Procedure, and have served at least one prior felony commitment at a state or federal correctional institution. Or have been sentenced as a habitual, violent habitual, violent career criminal, or a sexual predator must be supervised under this program. This is NOT a discretionary early release program. When the qualifying offender is released by virtue of awards of gain time, the Commission imposes appropriate terms and conditions of supervision until the end of the court-imposed sentence.

Confidential Case Analysis: The staff report for a clemency application prepared by the parole examine, and adopted by a majority of commissioners as an advisory recommendation for the BOEC.

Consecutive Sentence: Two or more sentences of jail time to be served one after another.

Deportation: Deportation (also called "removal") occurs when the federal government formally removes an alien from the United States for violations of a number of immigration or criminal laws.

Detainer: The act of keeping a person against his will, or of keeping goods or property.

Effective Interview: The purpose of this hearing is to determine if the inmate will be granted parole. The commission can elect to grant parole, extend the Presumptive Parole Release Date

(PPRD) or decline to authorize parole (placing the PPRD in a suspended status).

Effective Parole Release Date (EPRD): The actual parole release date authorized by the commission.

Exceptional Merit: The standard under Rule 17 to get a clemency case expedited.

Executive Clemency: The clemency function is an act of mercy that absolves an individual from all or any part of the punishment that the law imposes. This is a power to grant full or conditional pardons, or commute punishment. There are rules for these lengthy procedures, and these powers are vested in the governor only with the agreement of two cabinet members who are also statewide elected officials. There are eight (8) types of clemency:

1. **Full Pardon:** Unconditionally releases a person from punishment, and forgives guilt for any Florida convictions. It restores to an applicant all of the rights of citizenship possessed by the person before his or her conviction, including the right to own, possess, or use firearms.

2. **Pardon Without Firearm Authority:** Releases a person from punishment and forgives guilt. It entitles an applicant to all of the rights of citizenship enjoyed by the person before his or her conviction, except the specific authority to own, possess, or use firearms.

3. **Pardon for Misdemeanor:** Releases a person from punishment and forgives guilt.

4. **Commutation of Sentence:** An adjustment to an applicant's penalty to one less severe. It does not restore any civil rights, nor does it restore the authority to own, possess, or use firearms.

5. **Remission of Fines and Forfeitures:** Suspends, reduces, or removes fines or forfeitures.

6. Specific Authority to Own, Possess or Use a Firearm:
Restores to an applicant the right to own, possess, or use firearms, which were lost as a result of a felony conviction. Due to federal firearms laws, the Clemency Board will not consider requests for firearm authority from individuals convicted in federal or out-of-state courts. In order to comply with the federal laws, a Presidential Pardon or a Relief of Disability from the Bureau of Alcohol, Tobacco and Firearms must be issued in cases involving federal court convictions. A pardon or restoration of civil rights with no restrictions on firearms must be issued by the state where the conviction occurred.

7. Restoration of Civil Rights (RCR): Restores to an applicant all of the rights of citizenship in the State of Florida enjoyed before the felony conviction, except the specific authority to own, possess, or use firearms. Such restoration shall not relieve an applicant from the registration and notification requirements or any other obligations and restrictions imposed by law upon sexual predators or sexual offenders.

8. Restoration of Alien Status under Florida Law: Restores to an applicant, who is not a citizen of the United States, such rights enjoyed by him or her under the authority of the State of Florida, which were lost as a result of a conviction of any crime that is a felony or would be a felony under Florida law, except the specific authority to own, possess, or use firearms. However, restoration of these rights shall not affect the immigration status of the applicant (i.e., a certificate evidencing Restoration of Alien Status Under Florida Law shall not be a ground for relief from removal proceedings initiated by the United States Immigration and Naturalization Service).

Extraordinary Interview: When the Presumptive Parole Release date is in suspended status, the inmate receives an Extraordinary Interview. The purpose of this hearing is to determine if the inmate's Presumptive Parole Release Date (PPRD) should be removed from a suspended status. The Commission can elect to make no change in the (PPRD), or establish an Effective Parole Release Date (EPRD) within the next two years.

Extraordinary Review: A further examination by the Commission of the entire record in an inmate's case following the Commission's decision declining to authorize an Effective Parole Release Date.

Faith- and Character-Based Institutions (FCBIs): Entire correctional facilities devoted to the Faith- and Character-Based Correctional Initiative. Eligible inmates volunteer for FCBIs without regard to religion and can choose among secular or religious programming.

FCOR: Florida Commission on Offender Review.

FDOC: Florida Department of Corrections.

Felon: A person who has been convicted of a felony, which is a crime punishable by death or a term in state or federal prison.

Felony: Crime sufficiently serious to be punishable by death or a term in state or federal prison, as distinguished from a misdemeanor which is only punishable by confinement to county or local jail and/or a fine.

Felony Murder Rule: As used in Florida, this rule states that anyone involved in certain felonies (armed robbery, kidnapping, rape) -- and if in the commission of that felony, no matter their level of involvement, a death occurs -- all people involved in the felony will be charged with First Degree Murder and sentenced to Life Without the Possibility of Parole or the Death Penalty, the only two options for sentencing.

First Degree Murder: The unlawful killing of a human being when premeditated, or when committed by a person engaged in an unlawful act as defined in s. 782.04. First degree murder constitutes a capital felony.

Florida Commission on Offender Review: A group of three commissioners who make post release decisions affecting inmates and ex-offenders. The Commission functions as a quasi-judicial body. It also investigates clemency applications and makes advisory recommendations.

Florida Department of Corrections: The department charged with oversight of Florida inmates in its state prisons (including seven private prisons), and supervision of almost 146,000 active offenders on community supervision at probation offices throughout the state.

Florida Parole Commission: Created in 1941; in 2014 the name was changed to the Florida Commission on Offender Review.

Initial Interview: Parole will not be considered at this hearing. The purpose of this hearing is to establish a Presumptive Parole Release Date (PPRD) and the Next Interview Date (NID). The Commission evaluates many factors in establishing the PPRD.

Inmate: Any person under Florida Court Commitment to incarceration in any state or federal correctional facility, the Department, or to a county jail for a cumulative sentence of 12 months or more.

Institutional Conduct Record: The inmate's prison behavior including disciplinary reports.

Matrix Time Range: The appropriate range of months found where the offender's salient factor score total intersects with the offender's severity of offense behavior.

Mitigation: Reduction of the matrix time range, or the previously established presumptive parole release date.

Non-Advanceable Date: An inmate's release date that is restricted from continuous, monthly gain time awards over the entire length of sentence.

Objective Parole Guidelines: Established in 1981, there are six (6) main criteria upon which parole decisions are made.

Offense Severity Level: The statutorily assigned degree of felony or misdemeanor for the present offense of conviction.

Office of Executive Clemency: The coordinator and staff who administers the clemency process, including the quarterly public meetings at the state Capitol.

Parole: The release of an inmate, prior to the expiration of the inmate's sentence, with a period of supervision to be successfully completed by compliance with the enumerated conditions and terms of the release agreement as ordered by the commission. The decision of the Commission to parole an inmate shall represent an act of grace of the state, and shall not be considered a right.

Parole Supervision Review: The purpose of this hearing is to review the parolee's progress while on parole. The Commission may elect to make no change or modify the reporting schedule and/or conditions of parole, and schedule the next review date.

Parolee: An inmate placed on parole.

Parole Examiner: A commission staff member who interviews the inmate in prison, prepares a summary report, and makes a recommendation.

Perjury: The offense of willfully telling an untruth in a court after having taken an oath or affirmation.

Plea: A formal statement by or on behalf of a defendant or prisoner, stating guilt or innocence in response to a charge, offering an allegation of fact, or claiming that a point of law should apply.

PPRD: A Presumptive Parole Release Date (PPRD) is a tentative parole release date as determined by objective parole guidelines.

Probable Cause Affidavit: A sworn statement by a law enforcement officer that triggers an arrest. It describes the alleged facts and what specific laws were violated.

Probation: The release of a defendant for a period of supervision to be successfully completed by compliance with the enumerated conditions and terms of the release agreement as ordered by the trial court.

Program Participation: Inmate achievements and courses for work, education, vocational, spiritual, literacy and substance abuse programs.

Recidivism: A return to prison, which may be a result of a new conviction or a violation of post-prison supervision.

Revocation Hearing: This hearing occurs when an offender is alleged to have violated the conditions of his/her release. When the Commission finds the releasee guilty of a willful and substantial violation, it may order the violator returned to state prison to complete service of the original term of imprisonment.

Salient Factor Score: The indices of the offender's present and prior criminal behavior and related factors found by experience to be predictive in regard to parole outcome.

Severity of Offense Behavior: The statutorily assigned degree of felony or misdemeanor for the present offense of conviction.

Spousal Immunity: Under the Federal Rules of Evidence, in a criminal case the prosecution cannot compel the defendant's spouse to testify against him. This privilege only applies if the defendant and the spouse witness are currently married at the time of the prosecution. Additionally, this privilege may be waived by the witness spouse if he or she would like to testify.

Subsequent Interview: The purpose of this hearing is to determine if any change should be made in the Presumptive Parole Release Date (PPRD) and establish the Next Interview

Date (NID). The Commission can elect to make no change, reduce or extend the PPRD.

Supreme Court of Florida: The highest appellate court in Florida, comprised of seven (7) members appointed by the governor.

Trial: The examination of facts and law presided over by a judge (or other magistrate, such as a commissioner or judge pro tem) with authority to hear the matter (jurisdiction)

Waiver: The intentional and voluntary giving up of something, such as a right, either by an express statement or by conduct (such as not enforcing a right).

Work Release: The Department of Correction's Community Work Release program.

Work Visa: Temporary worker visas are for persons who want to enter the United States for employment lasting a fixed period of time, and are not considered permanent or indefinite.

ACKNOWLEDGMENTS

Many thanks to...

• Tallahassee lawyer and lobbyist Pamela Burch Fort, who in 2007 encouraged me to start writing and speaking about criminal justice issues.

• My publisher and best-selling author, Vic Johnson -- an Internet marketing expert and successful entrepreneur.

• Author and nutrition expert, Lisa Johnson, for her cover ideas.

• Graphic designer, Joni McPherson, of Iowa for creating the book's cover.

• Lynn McCartney, Sarah Bailey and Mary Jo Stresky for proofreading and editing.

• Harvey Morse, founder of the Florida Association of Private Investigators, for his review and suggestions for Chapter 2 on investigations.

• Marion Hammer, the Executive Director of Unified Sportsmen of Florida and a past president of the National Rifle Association, for reviewing and editing Chapter 5 on Specific Authority to Own, Possess or Use Firearms.

• Lawyers Neil Rambana (Tallahassee), McKenzie Hogan (Destin), and Stephen Binhak (Miami), experts on federal immigration law, for editing and helping write Chapter 9 on how clemency may impact immigration proceedings and decisions.

• Lawyers Bryan Gowdy (Jacksonville) and Ian Goldstein (West Palm Beach) for peer-reviewing and editing Chapter 14 on post-Graham/Miller-related court decisions and legislation.

• Public policy advocates Roy Miller, president of The Children's Campaign, and Dewey Caruthers, its lead research expert, for reviewing and editing Chapter 14's Civil Citations section.

• Deceased Tampa lawyer Marcelino J. "Bubba" Huerta, III, who referred me my first clemency case (firearm authority) in 1994.

• Governors Lawton Chiles (deceased), Jeb Bush, Charlie Crist and Rick Scott and their clemency lawyers: Mark Schlackman, Reg Brown, 5th DCA Judge Wendy Berger, Circuit Judge Vicki Brennan, Circuit Judge Rob Wheeler, Drew Atkinson, 1st DCA Judge Thomas "Bo" Winokur and Jack Heekin.

• Current and former Cabinet members, and their clemency lawyers and aides.

• Current and former parole commissioners and their staffs.

The author used publicly available information from various Florida government departments and agencies.

Information included in Chapters 4 to 7 and 14 previously appeared in legal articles published in *Florida Defender*, a magazine publication of the Florida Association of Criminal Defense Lawyers.

Information included in Chapters 6 and 7 also previously appeared in a legal article published in the *Journal*, a magazine publication of the Florida Justice Association.

Also By Reggie Garcia

HOW TO LEAVE PRISON EARLY

Florida Clemency, Parole and Work Release

Reggie Garcia

Lawyer & Lobbyist

More Praise for How to Leave Prison Early

"I just read your book ... and I am impressed. You gave a clear and concise explanation of clemency that was quite helpful."

— 24-year-old inmate serving 20 years for 2nd degree murder (4/14/15)

"As Florida's premier expert on early inmate release, attorney Reggie Garcia has written this much needed easy to read book and excellent guide for his primary intended audiences the inmate, their families and supporters. A must read."

— Hon. Bob Butterworth, Esq., Clemency Board member as four-term Attorney General of Florida 1987-2003 (5/26/15)

"Reggie Garcia has always been very professional in his appearances before the Florida Cabinet."

— Hon. Jim Smith, Esq., Clemency Board member as FL Secretary of State 2002-2003 and Florida Attorney General 1979-1987 (8/11/15)

"As a Clemency Board member for 10 years, clemency decisions were often difficult ones for me and my colleagues. However, these cases gave us an opportunity to approve citizens who earned mercy and a second chance. With his 20 years' experience, Mr. Garcia has the credibility to help the board make informed decisions. He is a trusted advocate."

— Hon. Tom Gallagher, Clemency Board member as Florida Chief Financial Officer 2003-2007 and Florida Treasurer 1989-1995 (7/8/15)

"Reggie Garcia has taken his years of successful experience and condensed them in this easy to read and remarkably helpful book. It is a must read not only for those incarcerated but also for the lawyers who help them and the decision-makers who consider their cases. "

— **Hon. Major Harding, Esq., former Chief Justice, Supreme Court of Florida 1991-2002 (5/4/15)**

"Among my proudest achievements are recognizing accomplished lawyers like Reggie Garcia (1985) who has a very unique and effective law specialty — to help get mercy, grace and justice for convicted felons who have earned a second chance from the governor and Florida Cabinet or the parole commission. Mr. Garcia's "How- to" book is well written, timely and mainly for people who cannot afford a lawyer. It will help inmates' families learn clemency, parole and other release options and strategies."

— **Fred Levin, Esq., the Trial Lawyer Hall of Fame and namesake of the UF Levin College of Law (4/19/15)**

"I really appreciated your book in that it was a very succinct and understandable explanation of a complicated process. It would act as a great handbook for lawyers to help educate their clients on this very cumbersome process and it gives a great overview of all the complexities. It is truly a how to and who with of the entire clemency process. Congratulations."

— **Mark M. O'Mara, Esq., Board Certified Criminal Trial Specialist, CNN Legal Analyst, and George Zimmerman's lawyer (7/16/15)**

"Reggie Garcia's very useful book comes at a time when large numbers of Floridians are caught in a dysfunctional criminal justice system. His wide experience has provided a base for good advice to those who are trapped in this system. I see the book as an important piece of the effort to fashion a system of smart justice."

— **Hon. Sandy D'Alemberte, Esq., former ABA President, FSU President, FSU Law Dean, and Founder of the Innocence Project of Florida (5/9/15)**

"This is a 'How To' book that should be required reading by inmates and lawyers seeking to obtain prison release."

— Morris S. Dees, Jr., Esq., nationally renowned civil rights trial lawyer and co-founder, Southern Poverty Law Center (4/28/15)

"Congratulations on publishing your great work. I'm quite sure it will be a great aid to those in need."

— Sister Mary Rinaldi, Development Director, Salesian Sisters of St. John Bosco, North Haledon, NJ (6/30/15)

Update of Chapter 2 and Appendix A
Clemency – Commutation of Sentence

When my first book, *How to Leave Prison Early: Florida Clemency, Parole and Work Release*, was published January 30, 2015, Florida Governor Rick Scott and the members of the Florida Cabinet, acting as the Board of Executive Clemency, had approved only one commutation (on December 12, 2013) for inmate Joseph F. Kelly (DC # 683781).

His offense was Trafficking in Cocaine and Conspiracy to Traffic in Cocaine in Broward County in 1999. His 20-year prison sentence was shortened to 15 years followed by five years' probation.

Two More State Commutations

At their quarterly meeting in Tallahassee on June 24, 2015, the Board approved two new commutations. These cases previously had been argued and taken "under advisement" (to be decided later) by Governor Scott. The two new commutations were for:

1. Inmate Ryan Holle (DC #126321). His offense was 1st degree murder, armed burglary and robbery with a gun/deadly weapon. He loaned his car to three people who killed an 18-year-old Pensacola woman in 2003. Mr. Holle was sentenced under the "felony murder" law to life, and 13 years under the burglary and robbery convictions. Despite opposition from the victim's family and prosecutors, this sentence unanimously was commuted to 25 years and ten years' probation.

2. Inmate Joshua Hunter (DC #528354). His offense was DUI Manslaughter after his truck accident killed a friend in Sarasota in

2009. The deceased friend's family supported the clemency. He was sentenced to 10.4 years, but his sentence was commuted to seven years, plus one year house arrest followed by seven years of probation (CFO Jeff Atwater did not support this commutation). Mr. Hunter was a popular high school football coach in Manatee County, and had good family and community support, including from the victim's parents.

Governor Scott described the two commutations as *"an opportunity to temper justice with mercy."*

While I didn't argue either of these cases, I informally advised both families after the hearings and while the cases were pending "under advisement."

Federal Commutations

A few weeks later on July 13, 2015, President Barack Obama announced he granted 46 federal prison commutations. In his personal letter to each inmate the president described the power to grant pardons and clemency as "one of the most profound authorities granted to the President of the United States."

He wrote (and said in a video statement) that clemency

> *". . . Embodies the basic belief in our democracy that people deserve a second chance after having made a mistake in their lives that led to a conviction under our laws" (underline added for emphasis).*

The president commuted the sentences of mostly non-violent drug offenders. It was the most presidential commutations in 50 years, since President Lyndon B. Johnson's term. With these new approvals, President Obama has commuted a total of 89 commutations, exceeding the number of commutations combined by Presidents Ronald Reagan, George H.W. Bush, Bill Clinton and George W. Bush.

More than 35,000 federal inmates, or 17%, have applied for clemency through the U.S. Department of Justice.

The policy reasons behind the commutations are:

1. These inmates were sentenced under harsh 1980's federal mandatory minimum sentencing guidelines, mainly in crack cocaine cases. If these cases occurred today, the sentences would be shorter.

2. To reduce costs and overcrowding in federal prisons.

During his time left in his second term, which ends January 20, 2017, President Obama is likely to grant more federal commutations.

A list of the commuted sentences can be found here:

https://www.whitehouse.gov/the-press-office/2015/07/13/president-obama-grants-commutations

There are 2.2 million people in prisons and jails throughout the country at a cost to taxpayers of approximately $80 billion. As such, criminal justice and prison reforms will continue to be a hot public policy and judicial issue, and one with a growing political consensus between conservative, moderate and liberal elected officials and advocacy groups.

###

www.ingramcontent.com/pod-product-compliance
Lightning Source LLC
Chambersburg PA
CBHW060026210326
41520CB00009B/1021